Joe Bonamassa
COLLECTION

CONTENTS

This book was approved by Joe Bonamassa

Photo Credit Karen Rosetzky

Transcribed by Paul Pappas and Jeff Jacobson

Cherry Lane Music Company
Director of Publications/Project Editor: Mark Phillips
Project Coordinator: Rebecca Skidmore

ISBN 978-1-60378-239-5

Visit our website at www.cherrylaneprint.com

ASKING AROUND FOR YOU

Words and Music by
Joe Bonamassa
and Michael Himelstein

Intro
Slowly, in 4 ♩ = 50

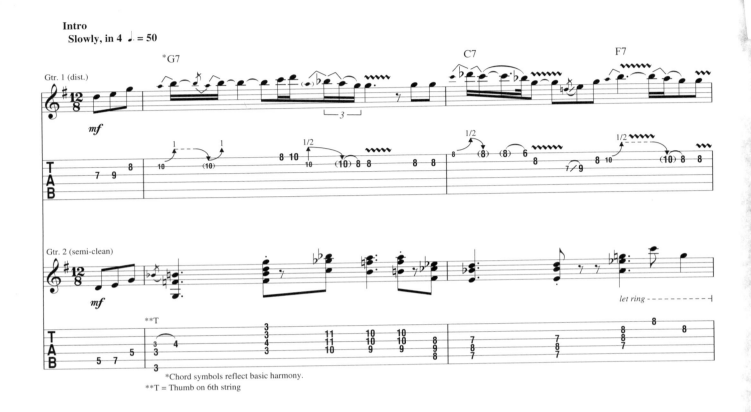

*Chord symbols reflect basic harmony.
**T = Thumb on 6th string

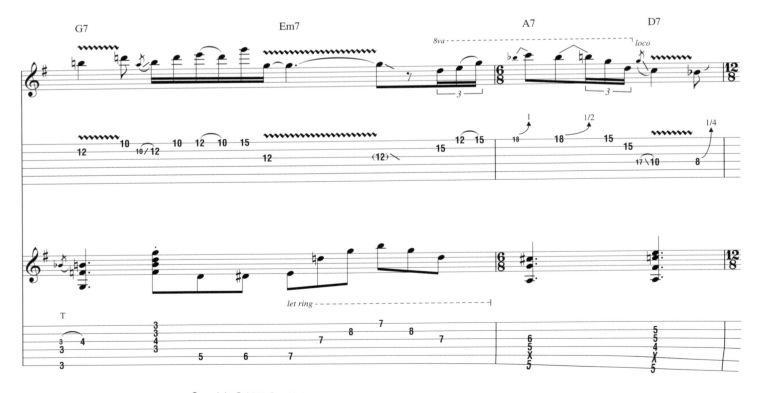

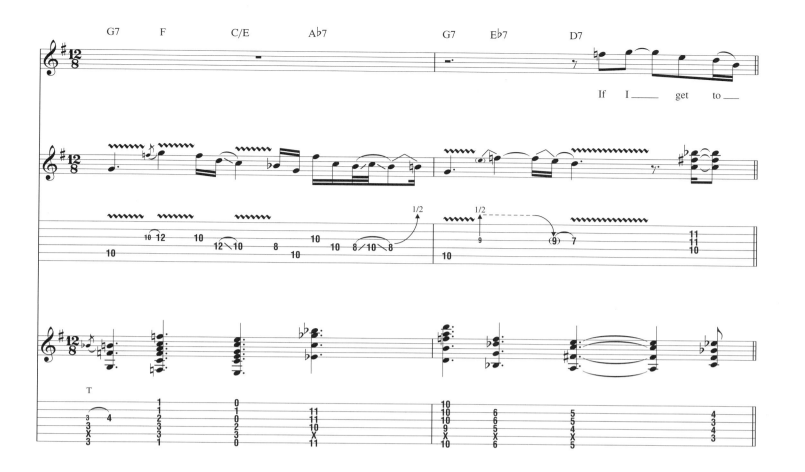

Verse

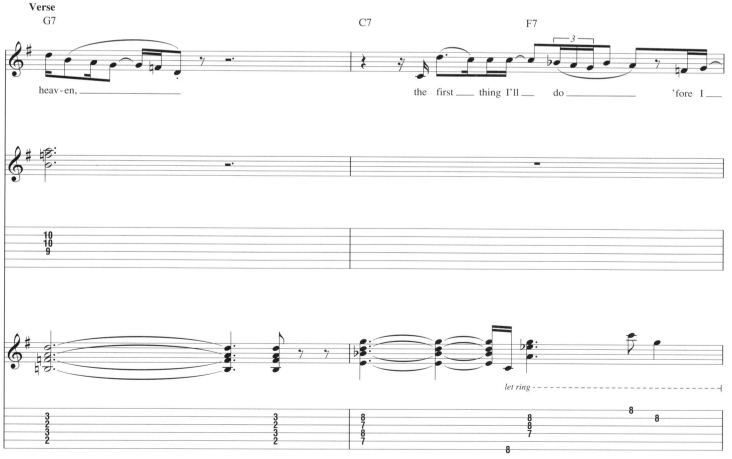

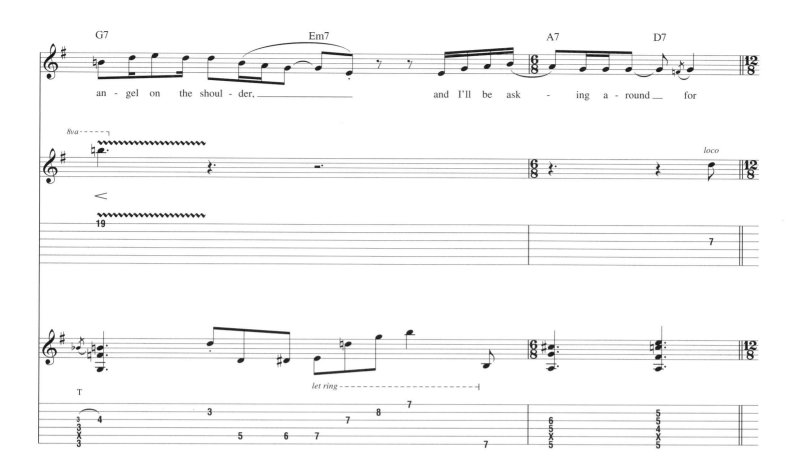

an - gel on the shoul - der, _____ and I'll be ask - ing a - round ___ for

Interlude

you.

She found _ a place _ up there _ where we all _____ can sit and talk a - while, _____

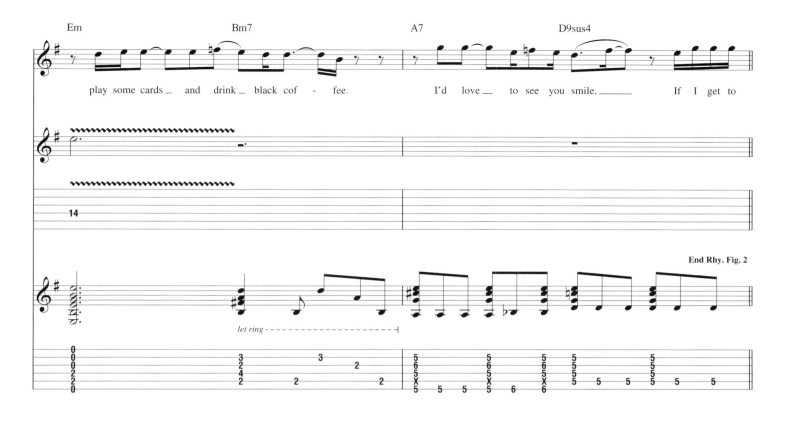

play some cards_ and drink_ black cof - fee.   I'd love_ to see you smile._   If I get to

Chorus
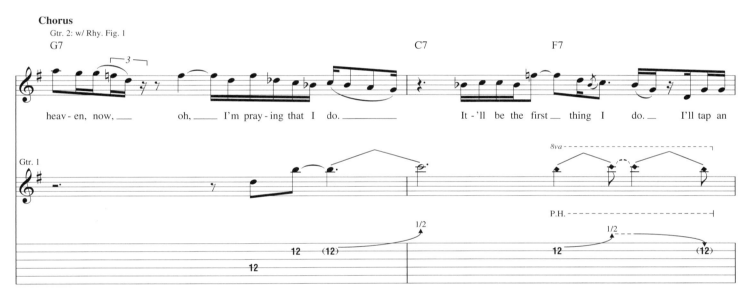

heav - en, now, _   oh, _ I'm pray-ing that I do. _   It -'ll be the first_ thing I do. _   I'll tap an

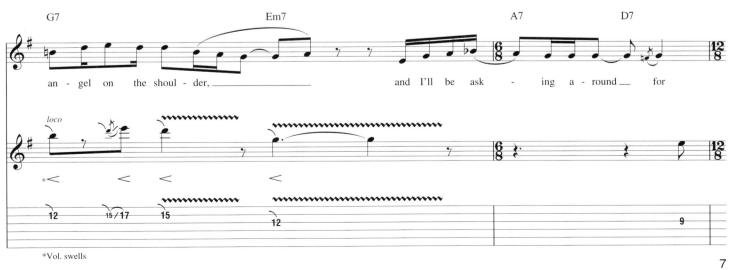

an - gel on the shoul - der, _   and I'll be ask - ing a - round_ for

*Vol. swells

7

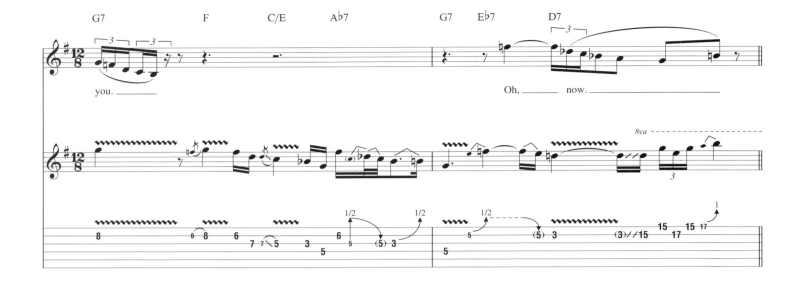

Oh, ____ now. ____

you. ____

Guitar Solo

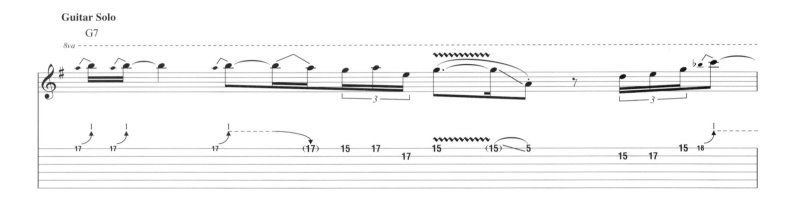

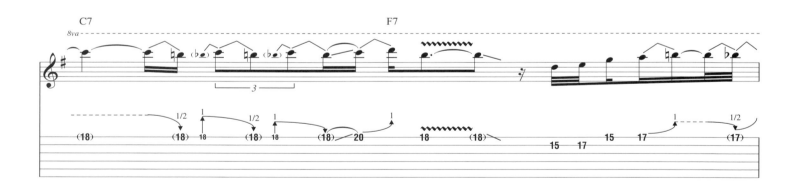

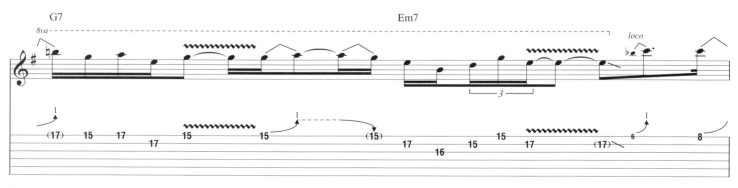

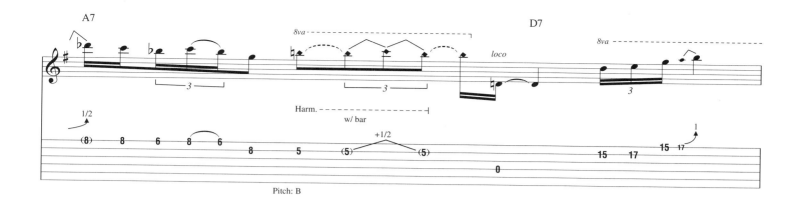

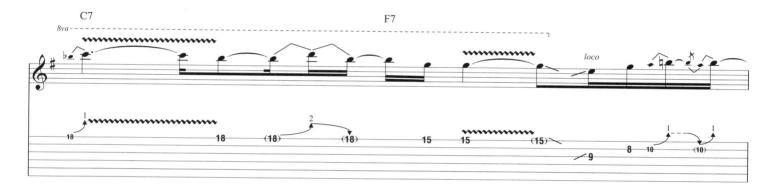

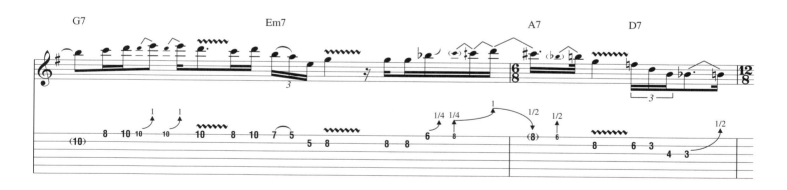

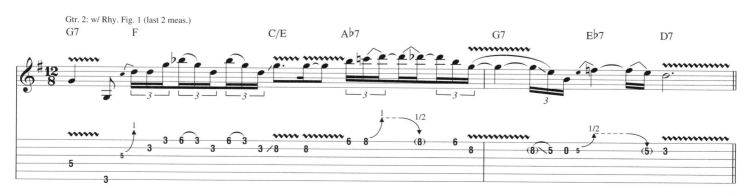

Bridge

Gtr. 2: w/ Rhy. Fig. 2

I'm sure you found a place up there where we all can sit and talk a - while,

rake - - - -

play some cards and drink black cof - fee. I'd love to see you smile. If I get to

8va

Chorus

heav - en, now, oh, I'm pray - ing that I do. I'll be the first thing I do. I'll tap an

Gtr. 1 8va

loco

Gtr. 2

let ring - - - - - - - - - - - - - - let ring - - - - - - - - - - -

10

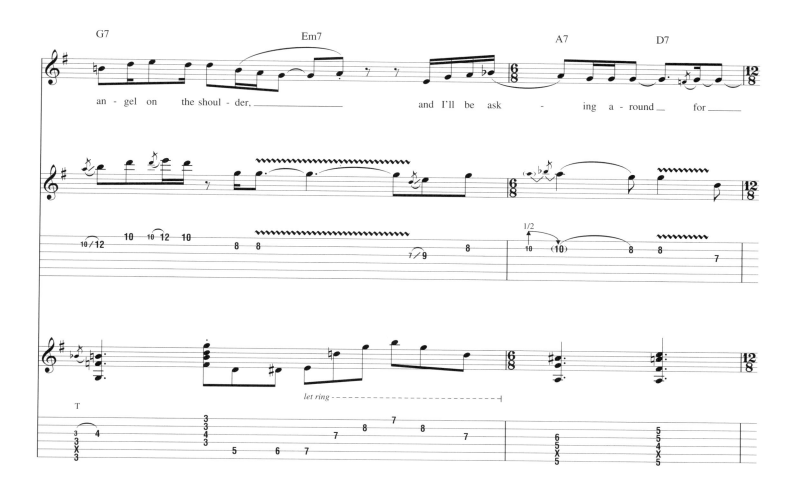

an - gel on   the shoul - der, _____   and I'll be ask - ing a - round__ for _____

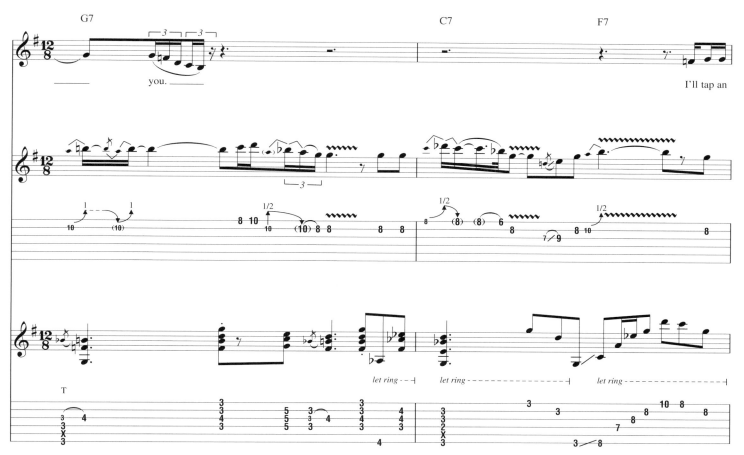

_____   you. _____   I'll tap an

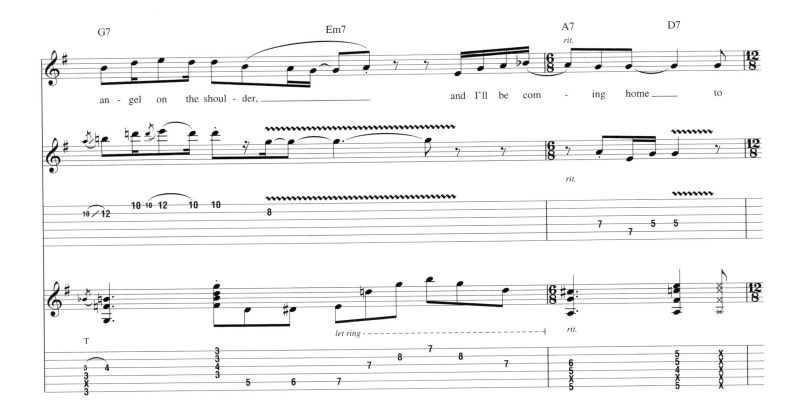

an - gel on the shoul - der, _____ and I'll be com - ing home _____ to

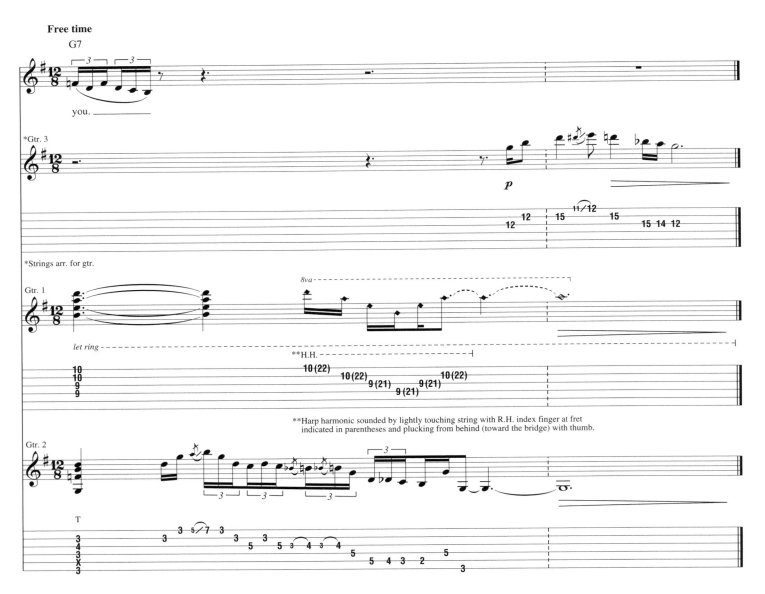

Free time

you.

*Gtr. 3

*Strings arr. for gtr.

Gtr. 1

**H.H.

**Harp harmonic sounded by lightly touching string with R.H. index finger at fret indicated in parentheses and plucking from behind (toward the bridge) with thumb.

Gtr. 2

BALLPEEN HAMMER

Words and Music by
Chris Whitley

*All music sounds a half step higher than indicated due to capo.

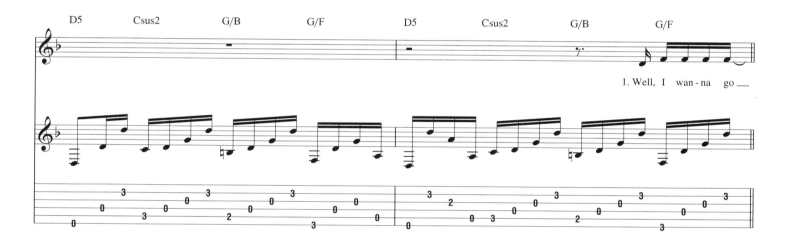

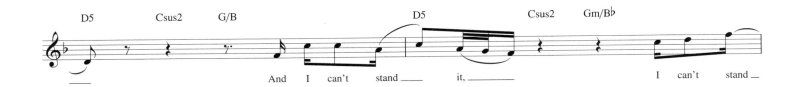

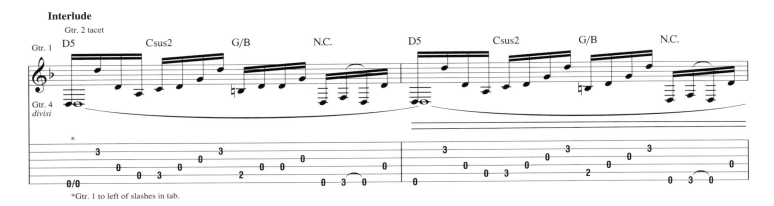

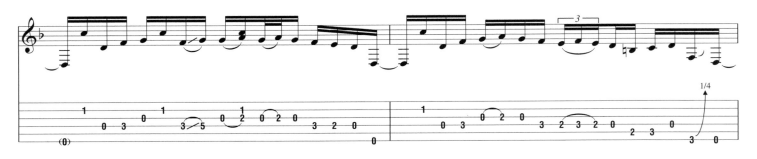

Verse

Gtr. 1: w/ Riff A (4 times)

3. No - where to - mor - row, __ a Sun - day rhyme. __

__ You know all __ good things __ come __ in their __ due time.

__ __ Put the ball - peen ham - mer __ right through __ that __ door,
* (Put the ball - peen ham - mer.) __

*Echo repeat

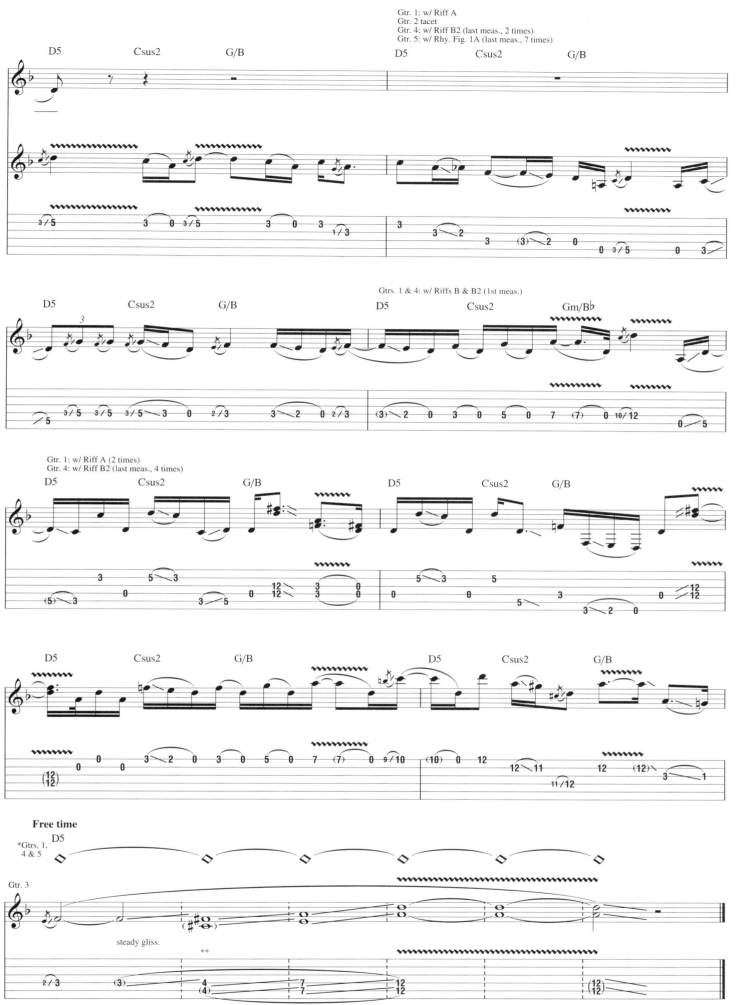

THE BALLAD OF JOHN HENRY

Words and Music by
Joe Bonamassa

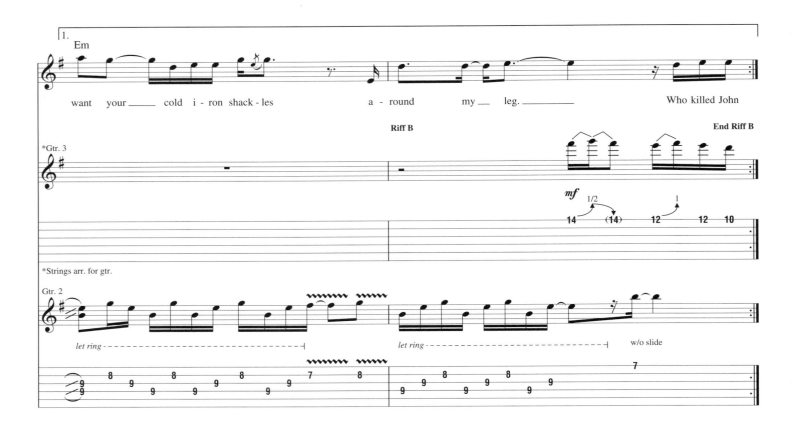

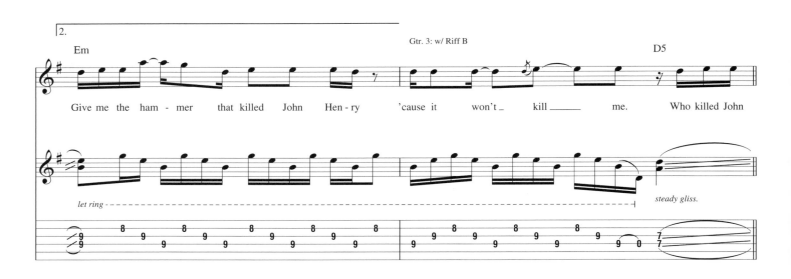

Chorus

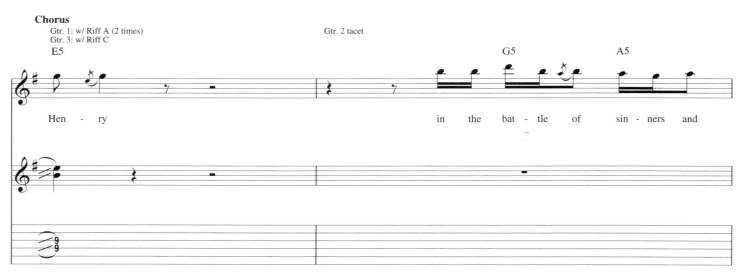

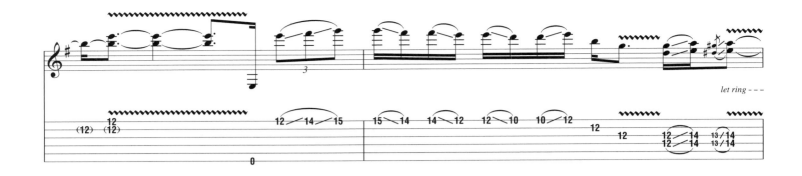

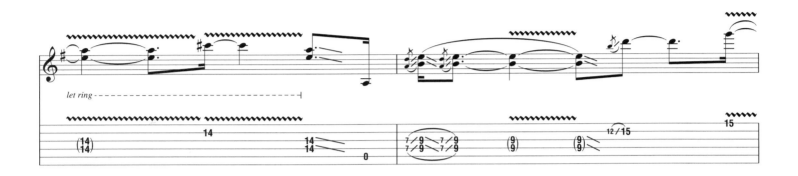

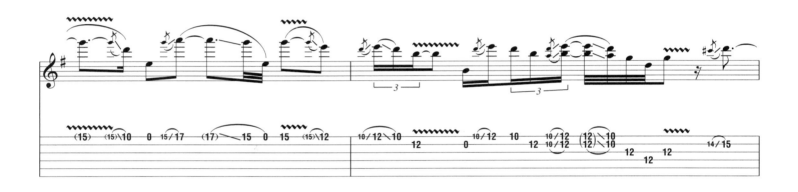

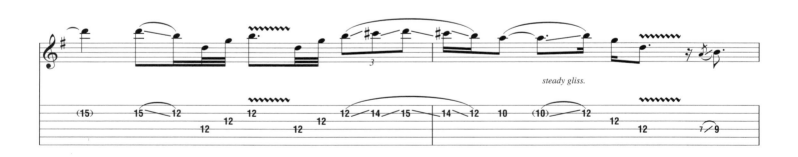

w/o slide

w/ slide

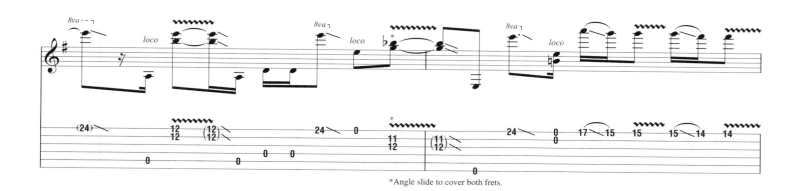

*Angle slide to cover both frets.

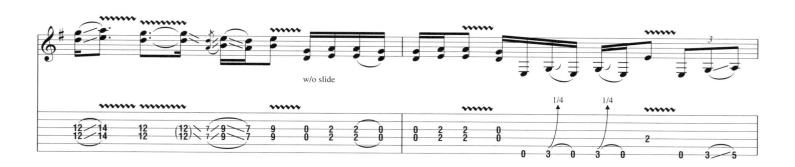

w/o slide

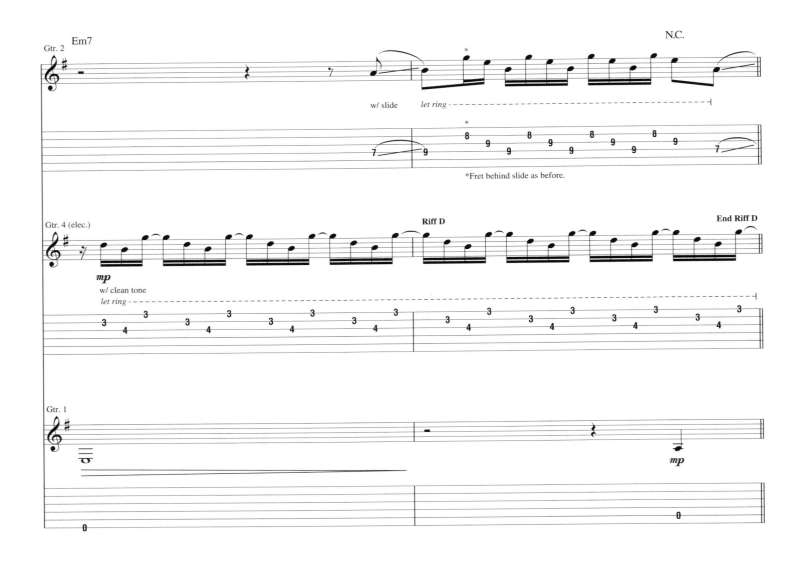

*Fret behind slide as before.

Verse
Gtr. 4: w/ Riff D (**8 times)

3. Take this ham - mer, car - ry it to the Cap - tain; tell him I'm___ go - in' home.___

**8th time, omit final tie.

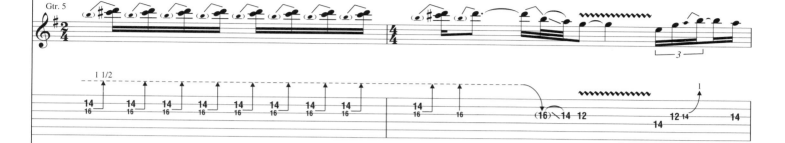

Repeat and fade

N.C.

BLACK NIGHT

Words and Music by
Jessie Mae Robinson

*Chord symbols reflect overall harmony.

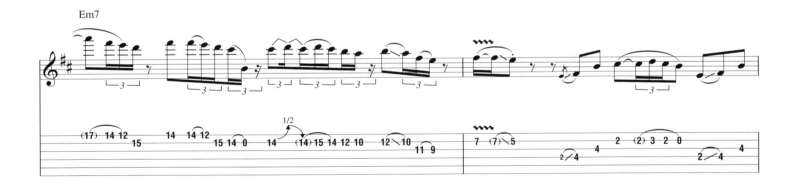

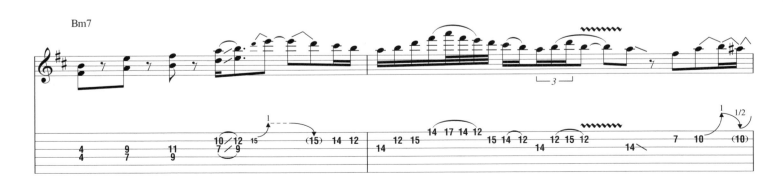

an-oth-er day ___ is ___ gone. ___

Guitar Solo

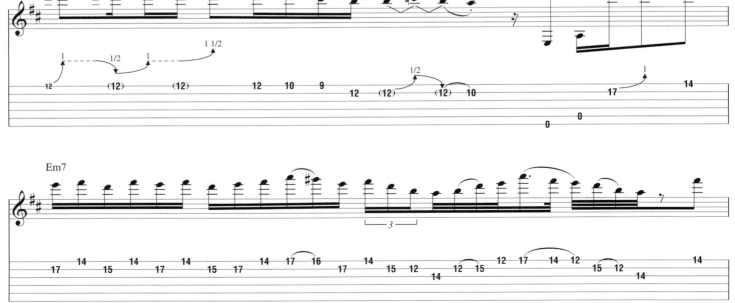

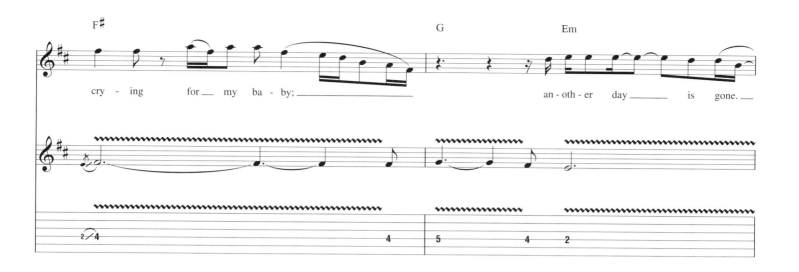

cry - ing   for — my ba - by; _____   an - oth - er   day _____   is gone. __

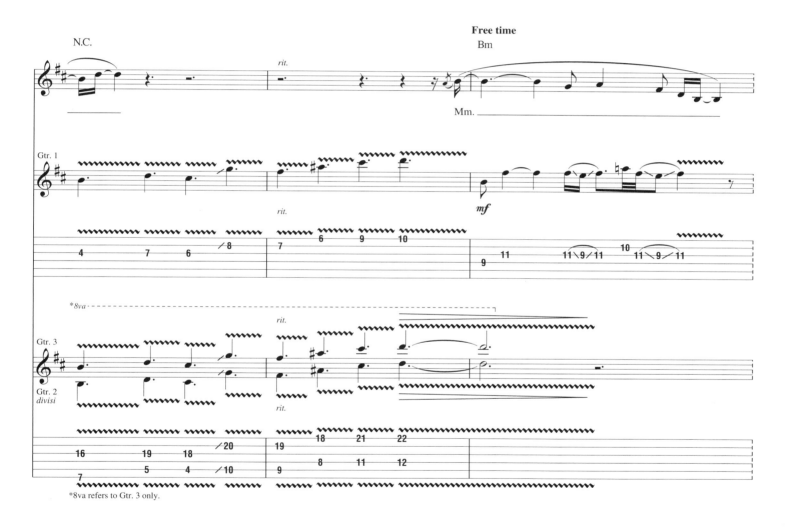

*8va refers to Gtr. 3 only.

BRIDGE TO BETTER DAYS

Words and Music by
Joe Bonamassa

Intro
Moderately slow ♩ = 88

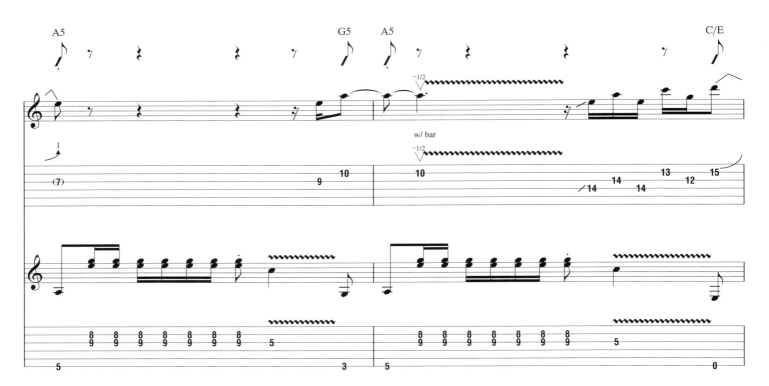

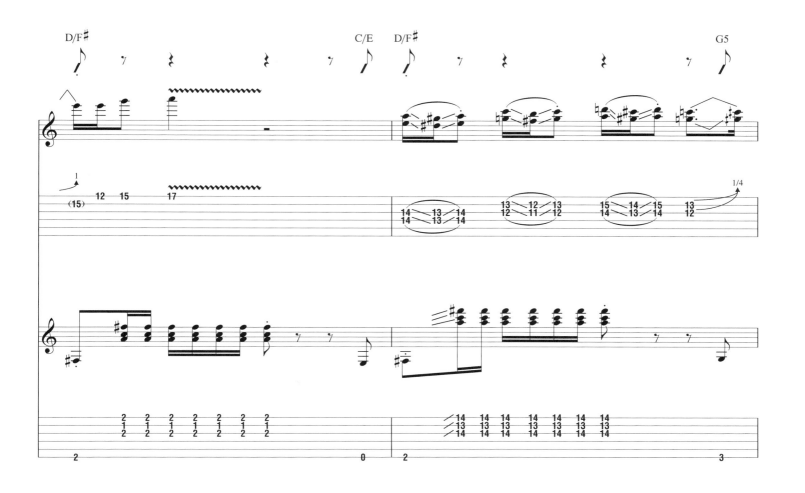

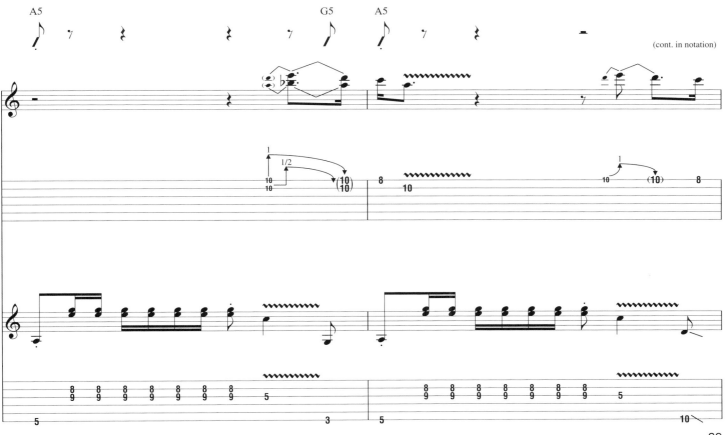

(cont. in notation)

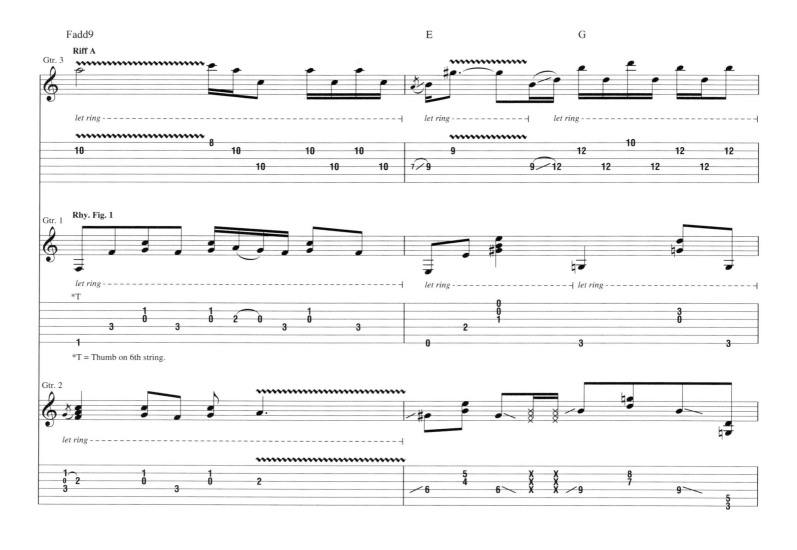

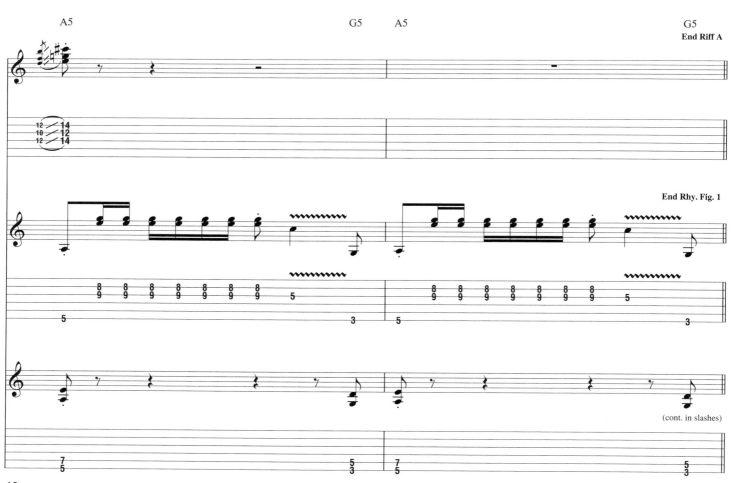

*Using a guitar with Les Paul style electronics, set lead volume to 10 and rhythm volume to 0. Strike the strings while the pickup selector switch is in the lead position, then flip the switch in the rhythm indicated to simulate the re-attack.

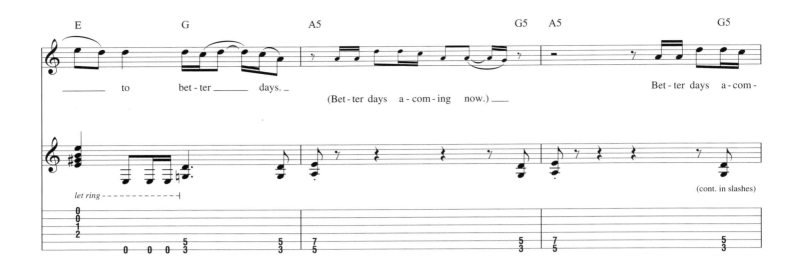

_____ to bet - ter _____ days. _

(Bet - ter days a - com - ing now.) _

Bet - ter days a - com-

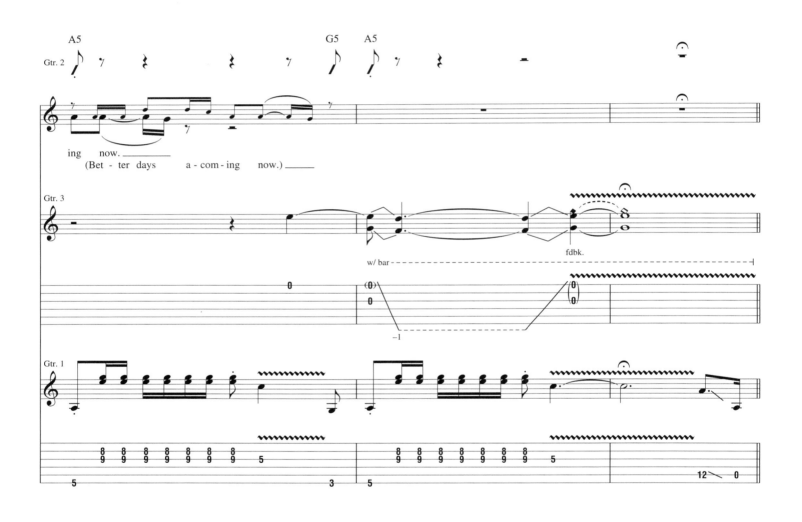

ing now. _

(Bet - ter days a - com - ing now.) _

Interlude
Gtrs. 2 & 3 tacet
N.C.
Rhy. Fig. 3

End Rhy. Fig. 3

Guitar Solo

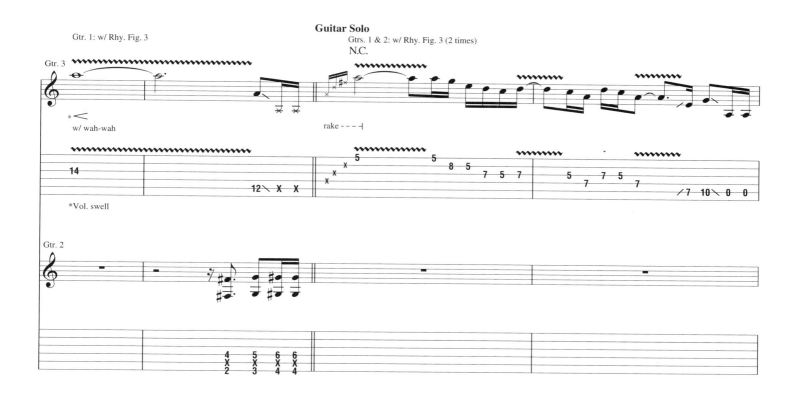

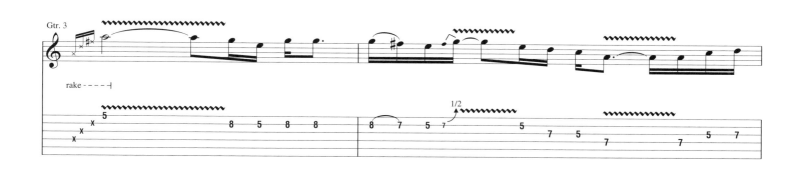

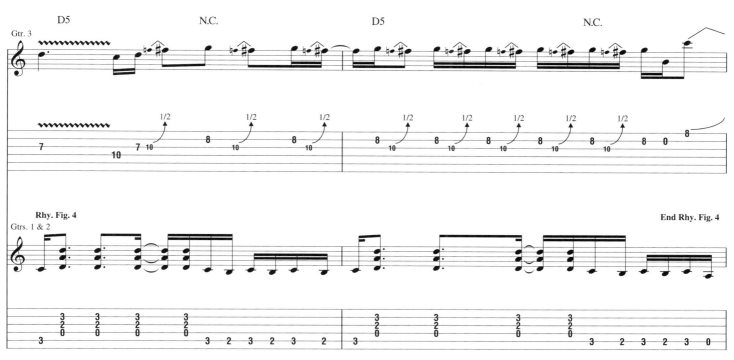

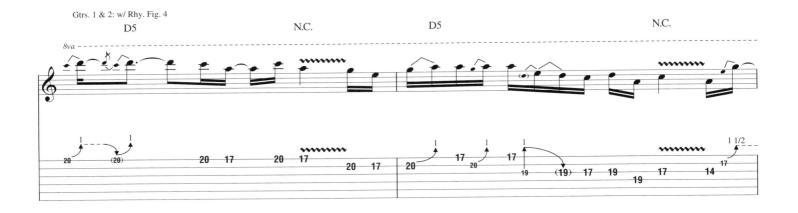

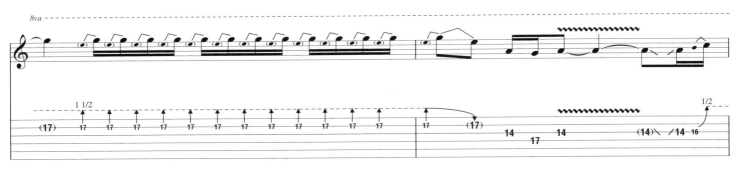

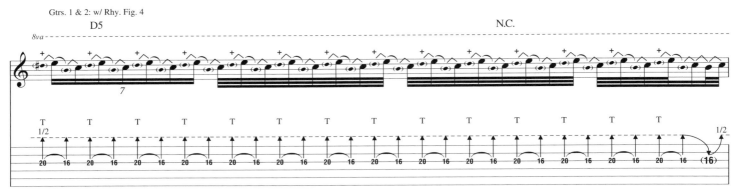

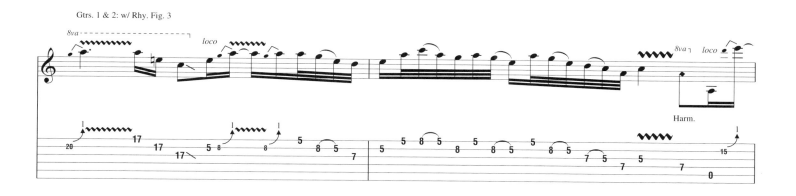

*As pitch descends, harm. gradually fades out and open string begins to sound.

Guitar Solo

Gtr. 1: w/ Rhy. Fig. 2 (1st 2 meas.)

Gtr. 3 tacet

(wah-wah off)

**8va refers to harmonics only.

Pitch: E   G   F#   E   F# G   E

*D7/F#   N.C.(C/E) *D7/F#   N.C.(G5)

*Bass plays F#.

(A5)   (G5) (A5)

Gtr. 3

Gtr. 1
divisi

Fsus2   Gtr. 3 tacet
              E   G5

Gtr. 1

let ring   let ring   let ring

**Gtr. 3 to left of slash in tab.

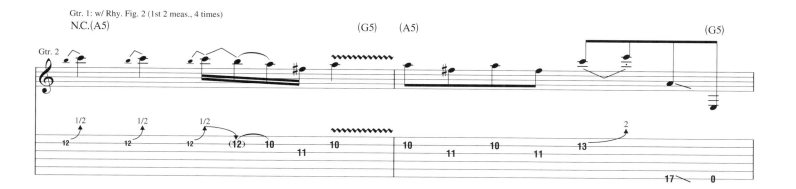

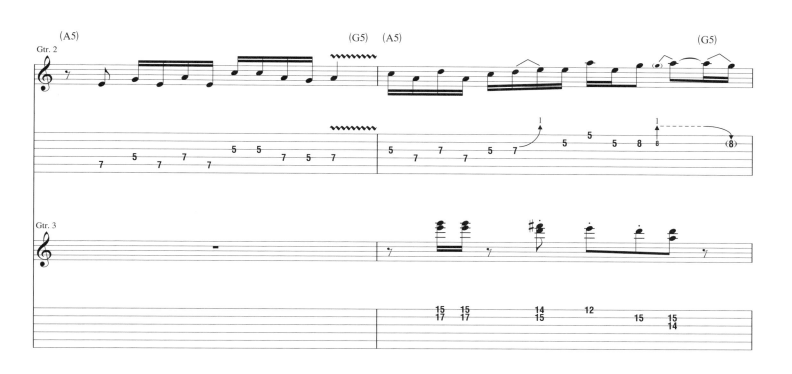

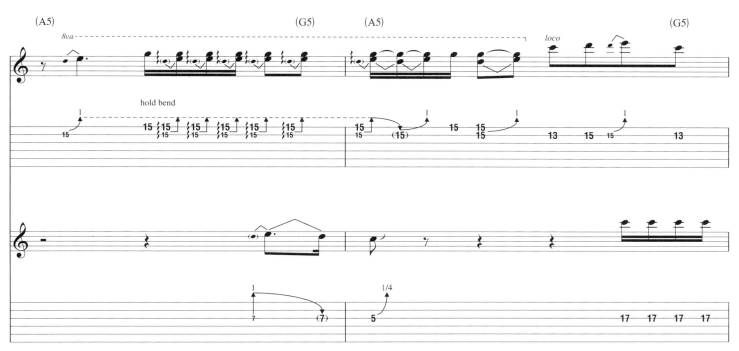

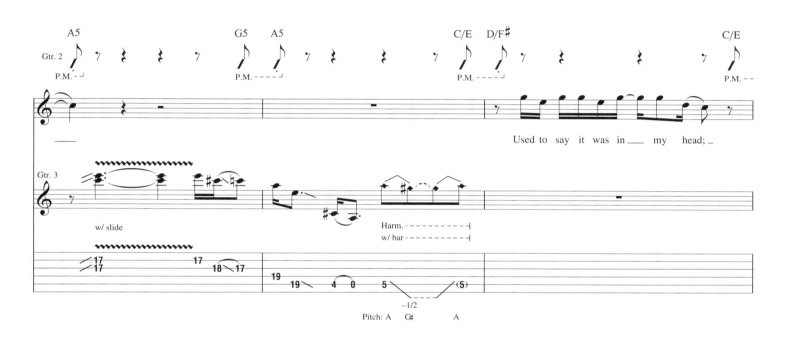

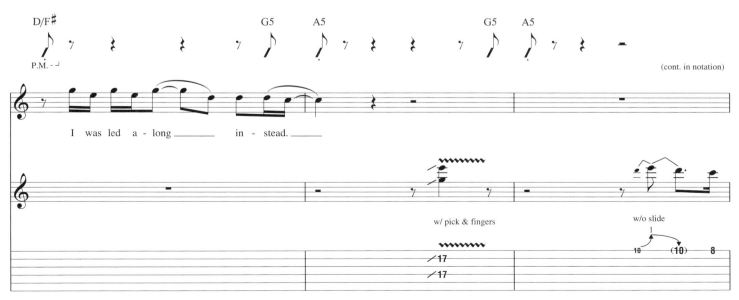

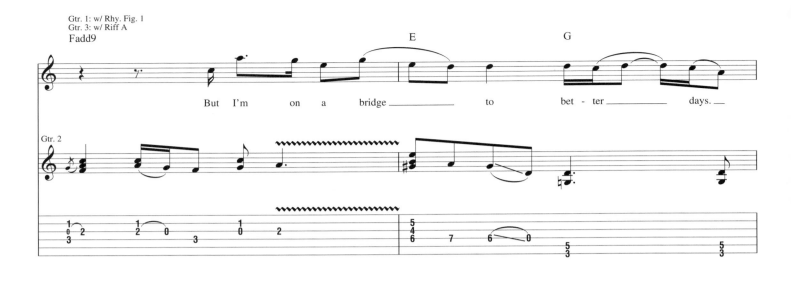

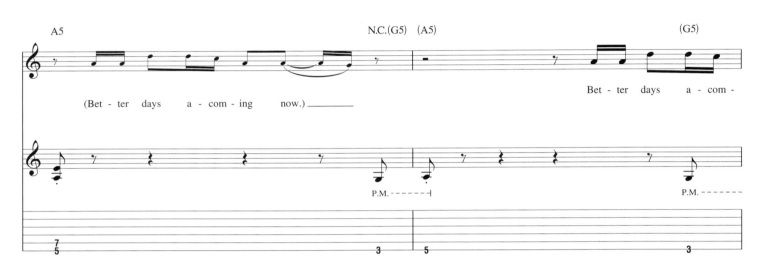

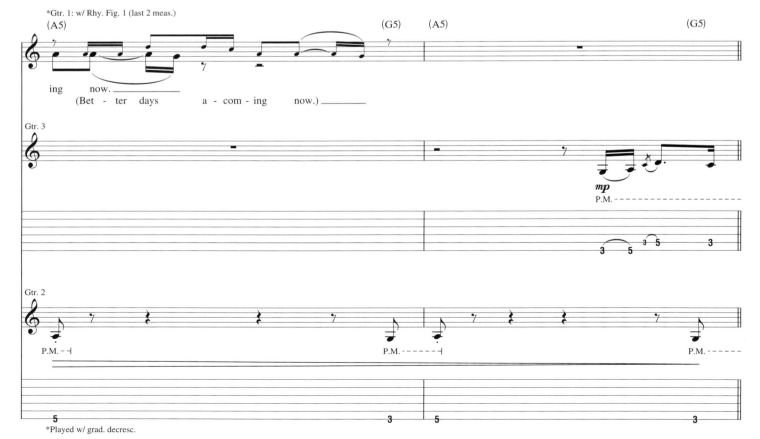

*Played w/ grad. decresc.

54

DIRT IN MY POCKET

Words and Music by
Joe Bonamassa and Jim Huff

Open E tuning:
(low to high) E-B-E-G♯-B-E

Intro

Moderately ♩ = 84

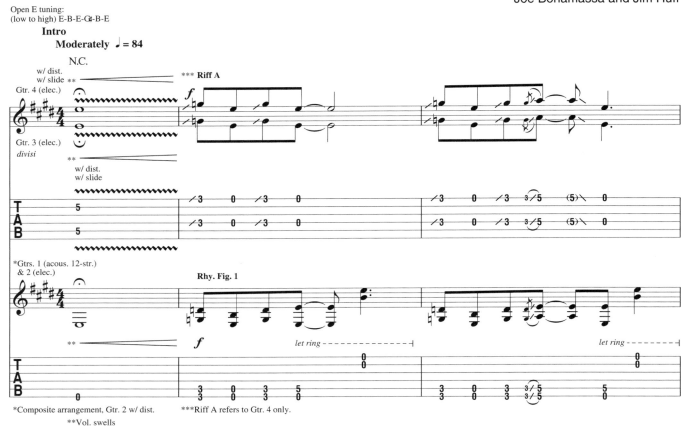

*Composite arrangement, Gtr. 2 w/ dist.
**Vol. swells
***Riff A refers to Gtr. 4 only.

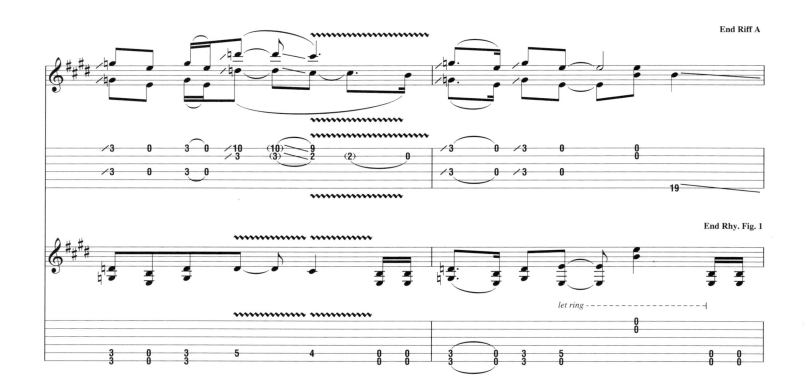

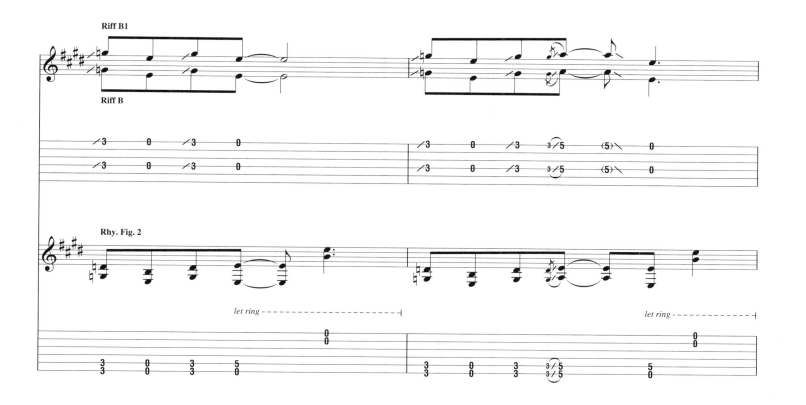

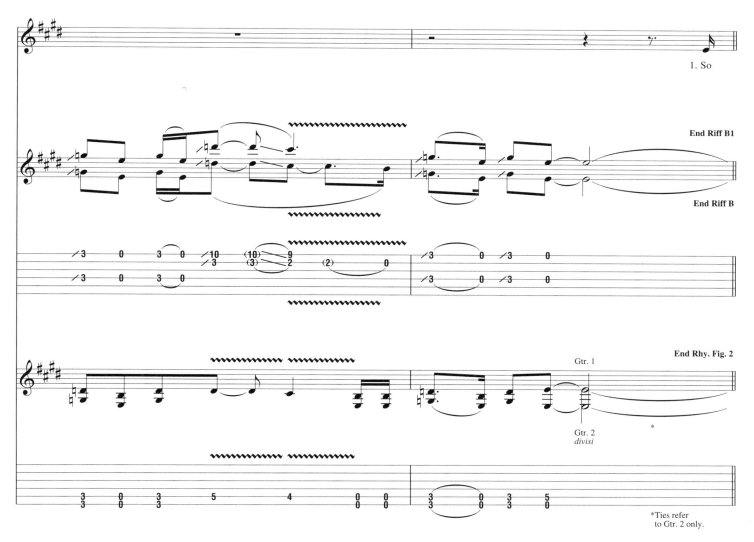

Verse

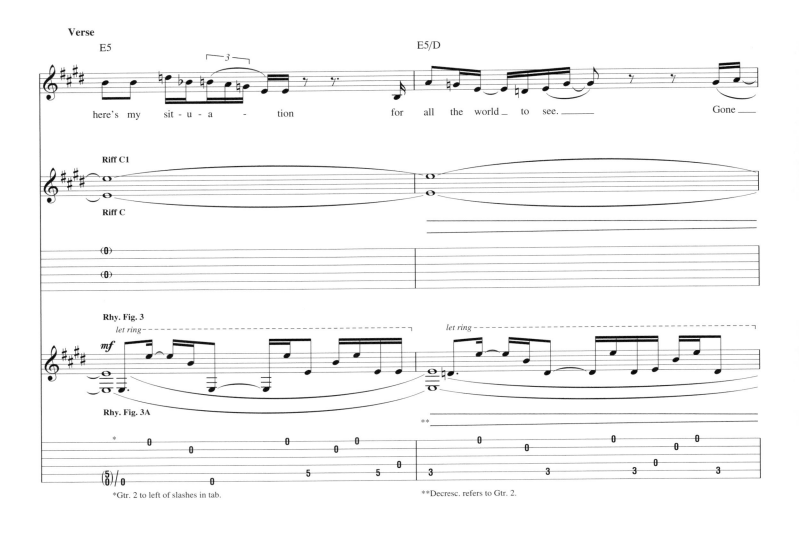

*Gtr. 2 to left of slashes in tab.   **Decresc. refers to Gtr. 2.

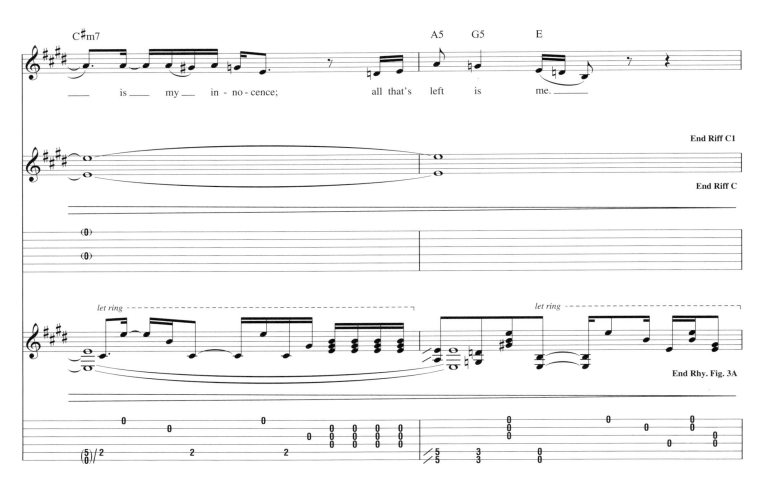

58

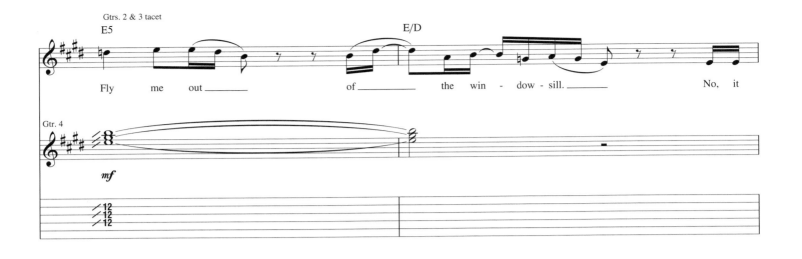

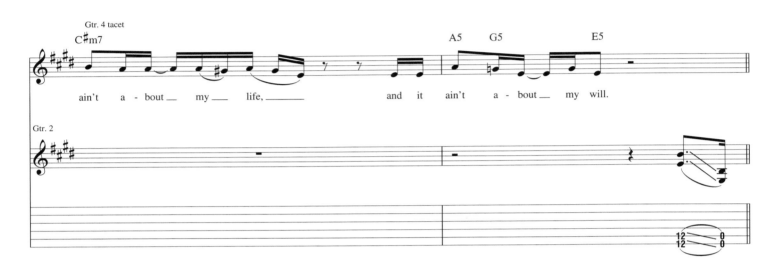

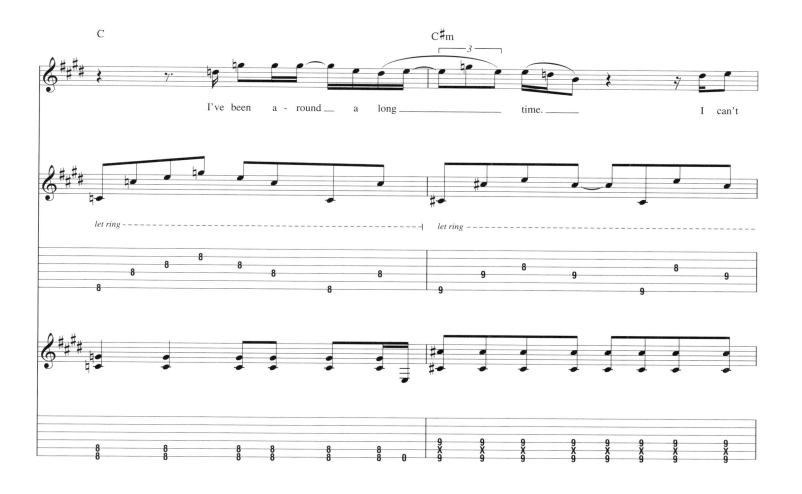

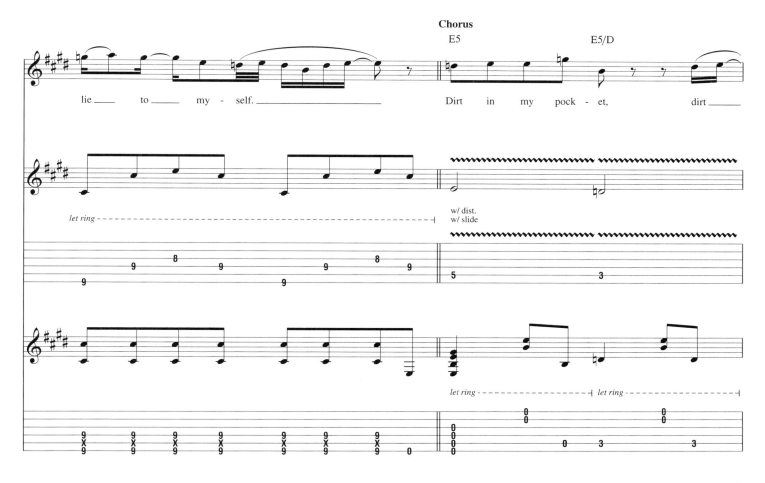

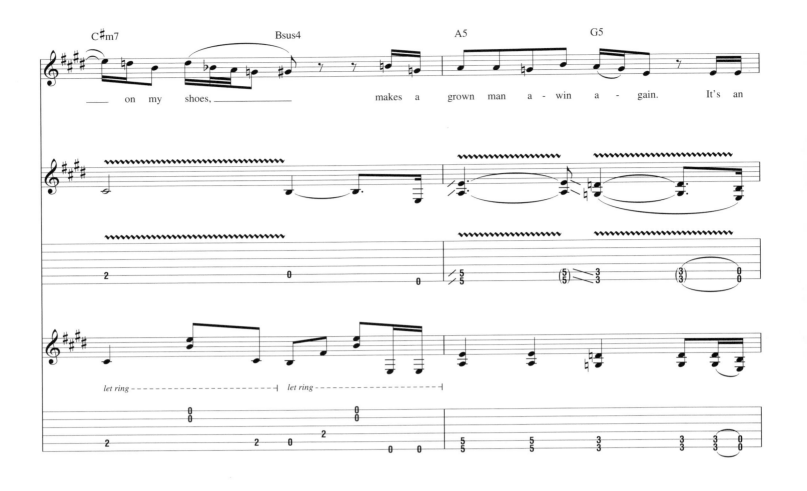

on my shoes, _____ makes a grown man a - win a - gain. It's an

eas - y man's _____ blues. _____ Dirt on my con - science, dirt _____ an

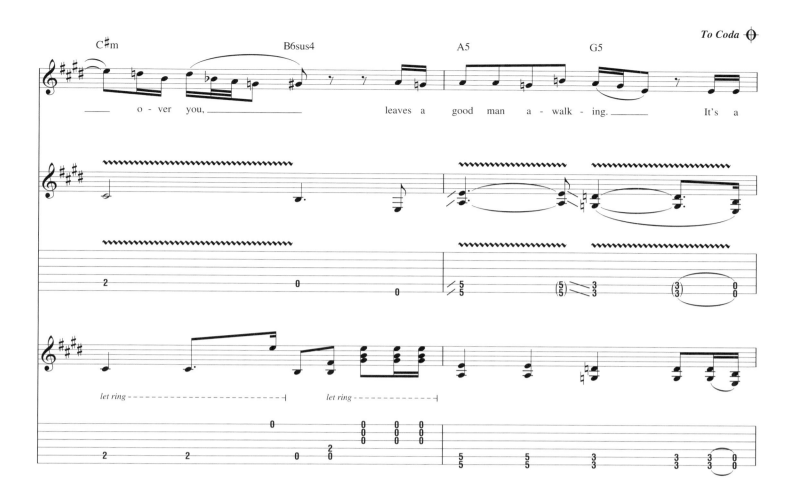

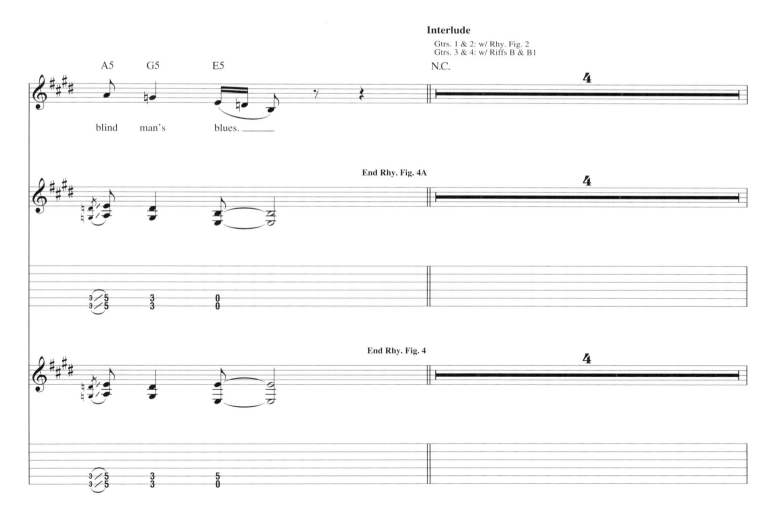

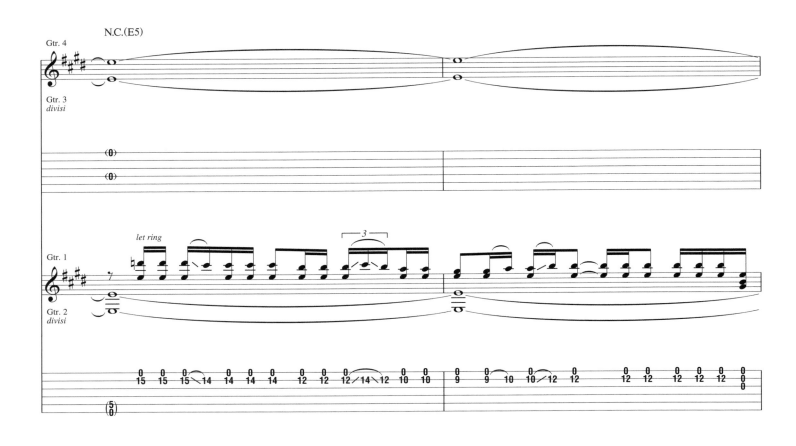

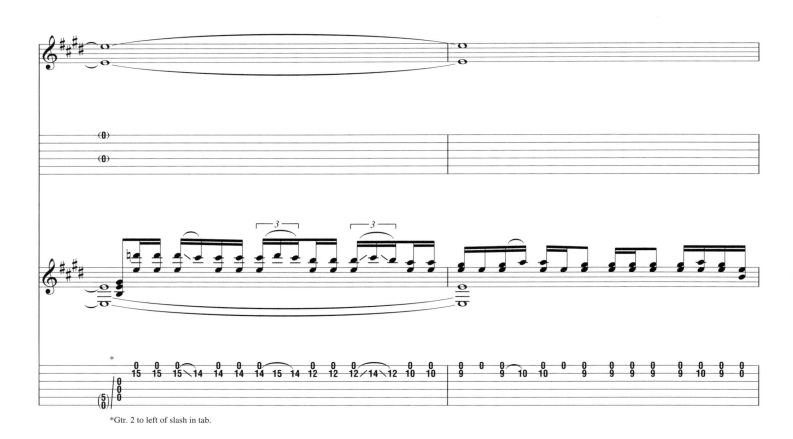

*Gtr. 2 to left of slash in tab.

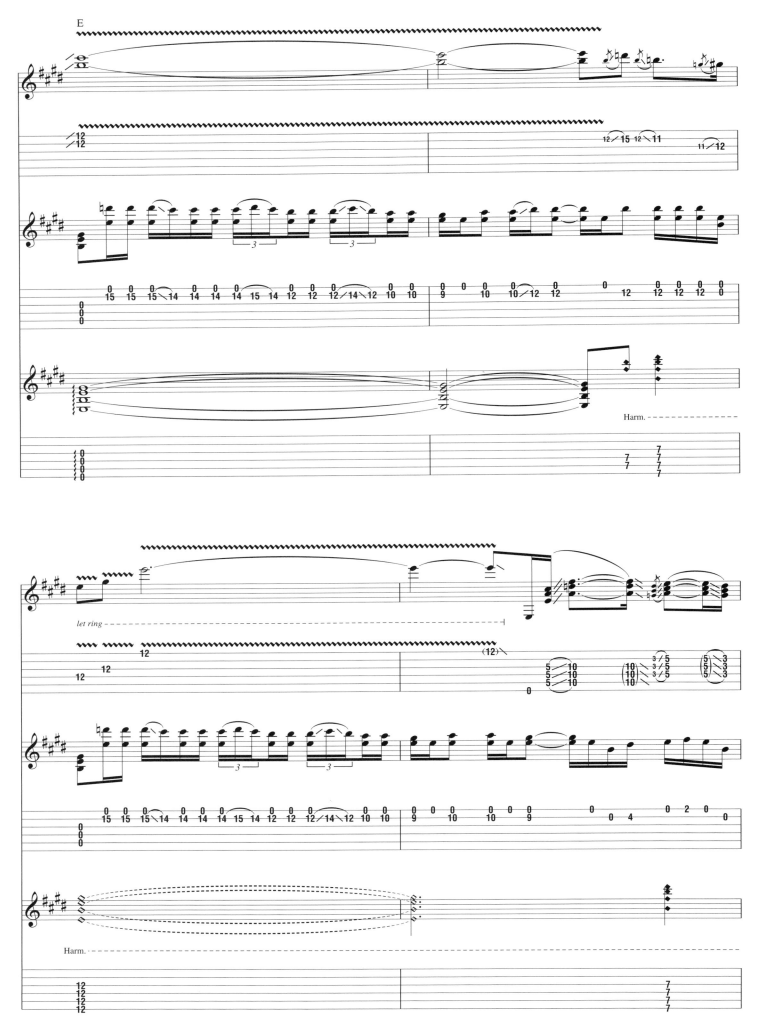

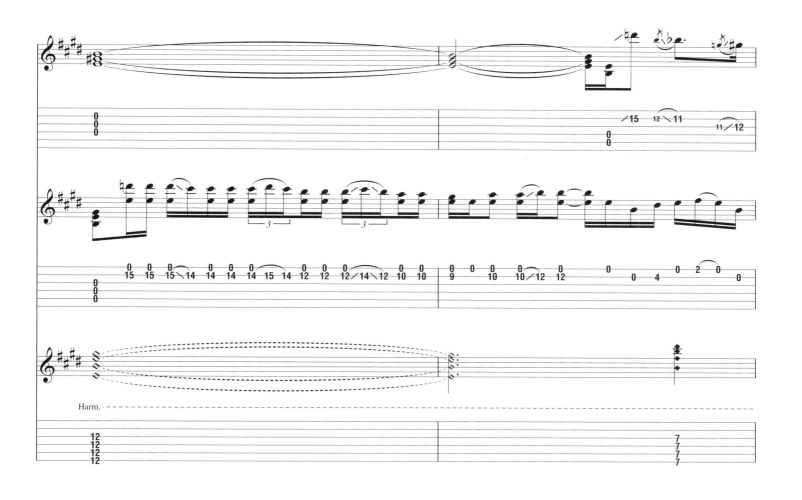

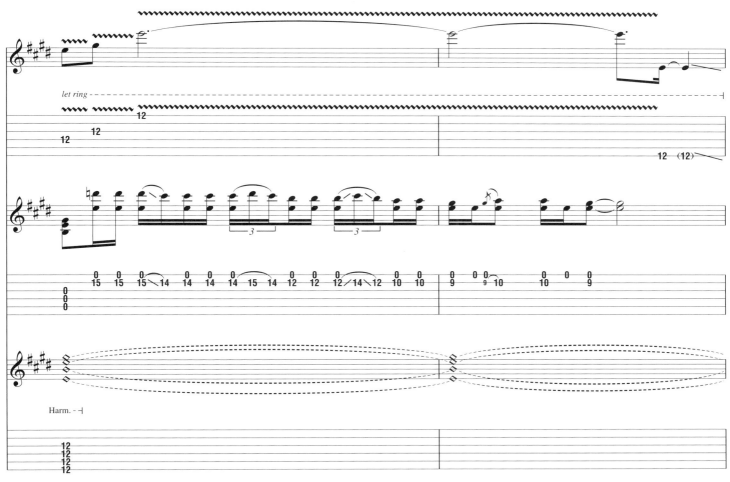

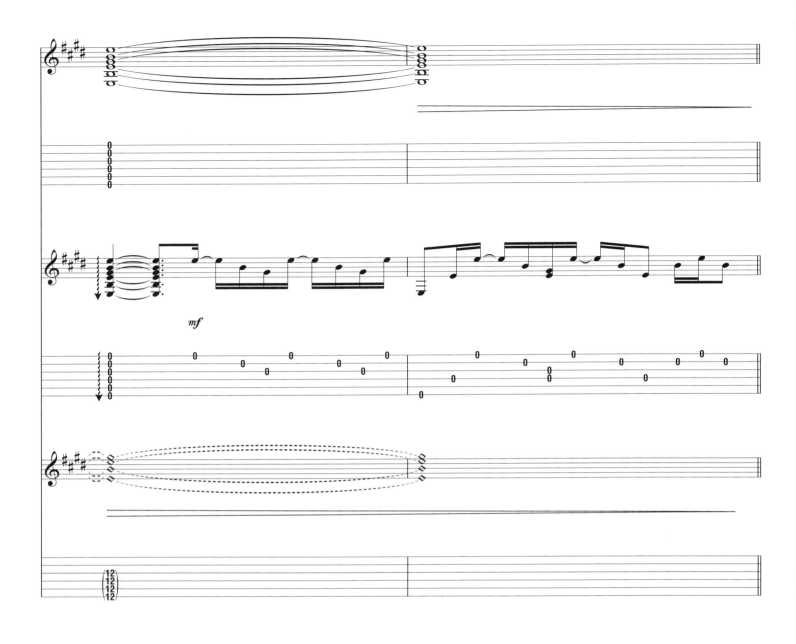

Verse

Gtr. 1: w/ Rhy. Fig. 3
Gtrs. 2 & 3 tacet

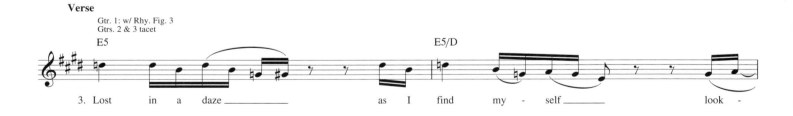

E5   E5/D

3. Lost   in a   daze _____   as I   find   my - self _____   look -

C#m7   A5   G5   E

- ing   for ___ new ___ ways ___   to   find   a   way ___ out. _____

Outro

Gtrs. 1 & 2: w/ Rhy. Fig. 1 (1 3/4 times)
Gtr. 4: w/ Riff A (1 3/4 times)

Hey. ___   Dirt in ___ my   pock - et, now. _

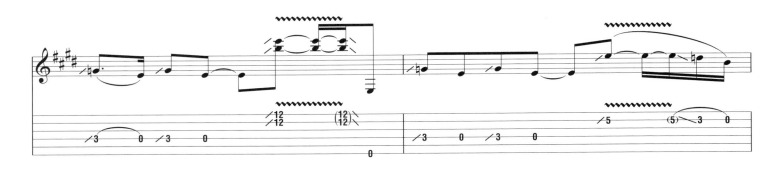

Mm. _____

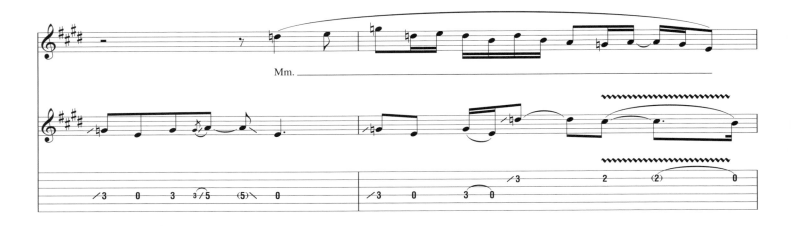

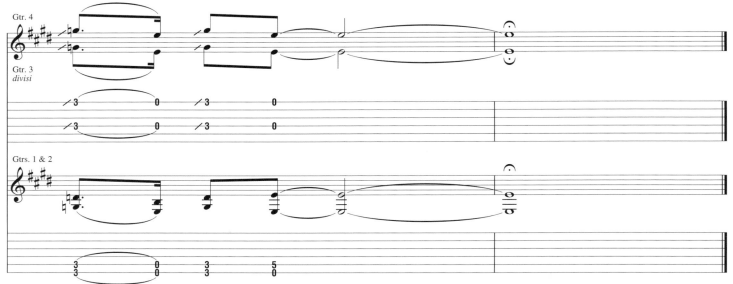

THE GREAT FLOOD

Words and Music by
Joe Bonamassa

*Chord symbols reflect overall harmony.
**Lower vol. w/ gtr.'s knob, thereby reducing dist. level.

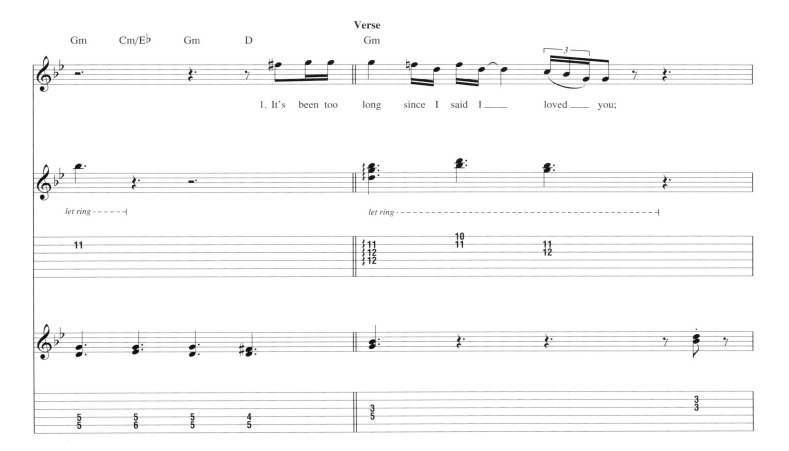

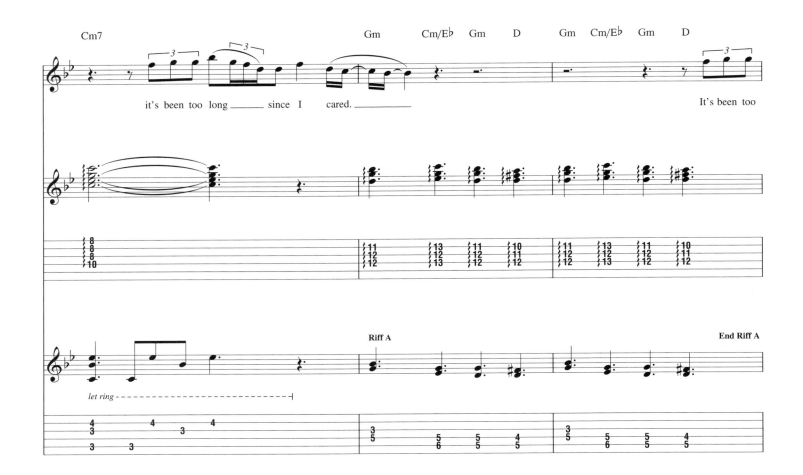

it's been too long _____ since I cared. _____   It's been too

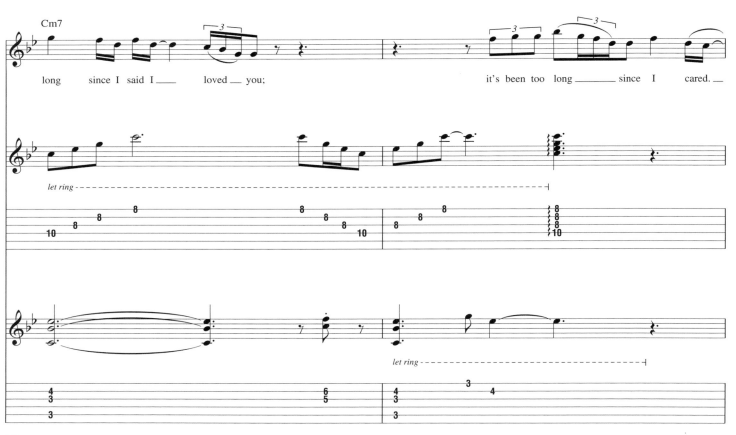

long   since I said I ____ loved ___ you;   it's been too long _____ since I   cared. __

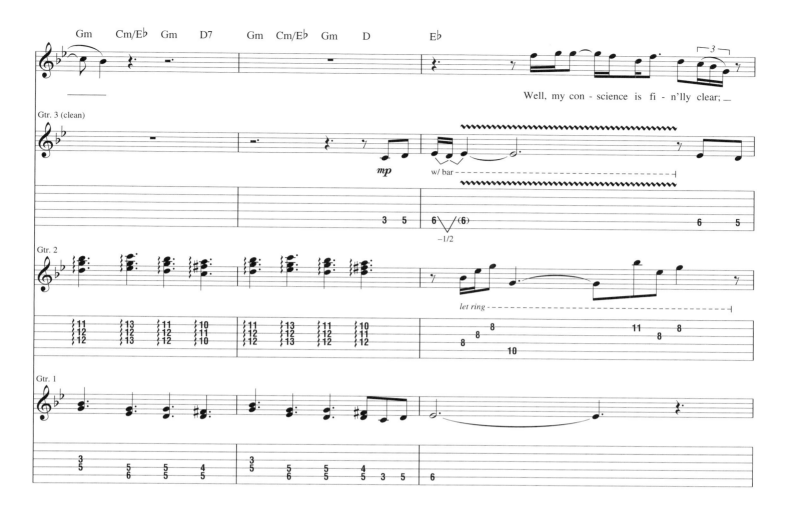

Well, my con - science is fi - n'lly clear; ___

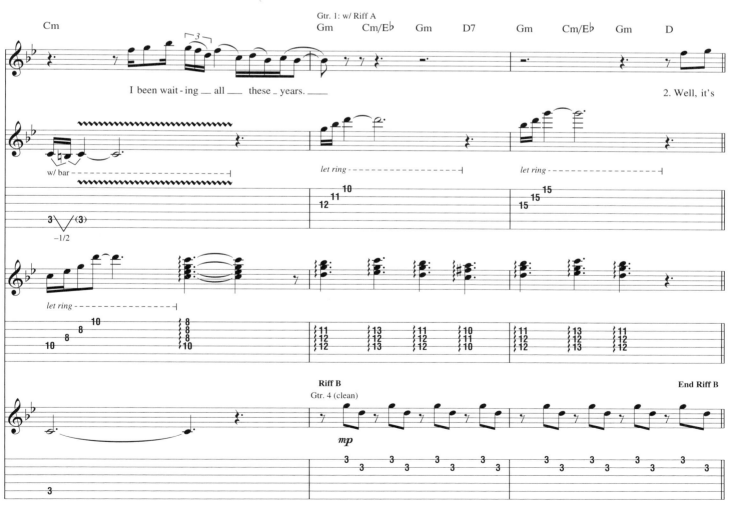

I been wait - ing ___ all ___ these ___ years. ___

2. Well, it's

Verse

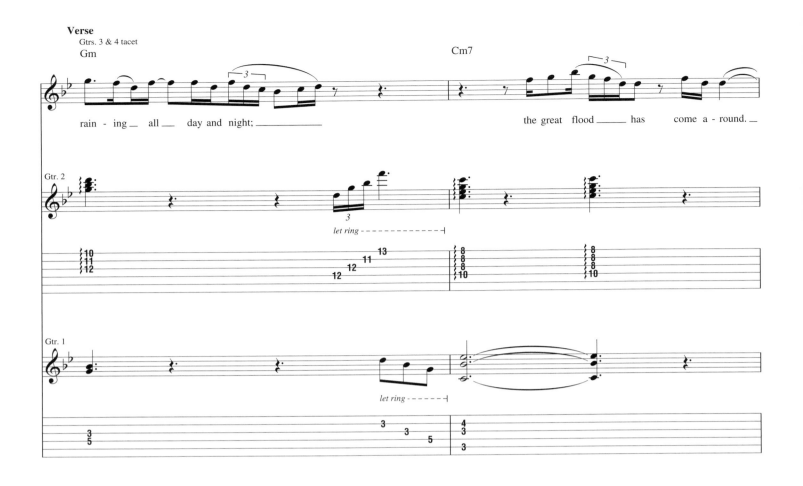

Gtrs. 3 & 4 tacet

rain - ing all day and night; the great flood has come a - round.

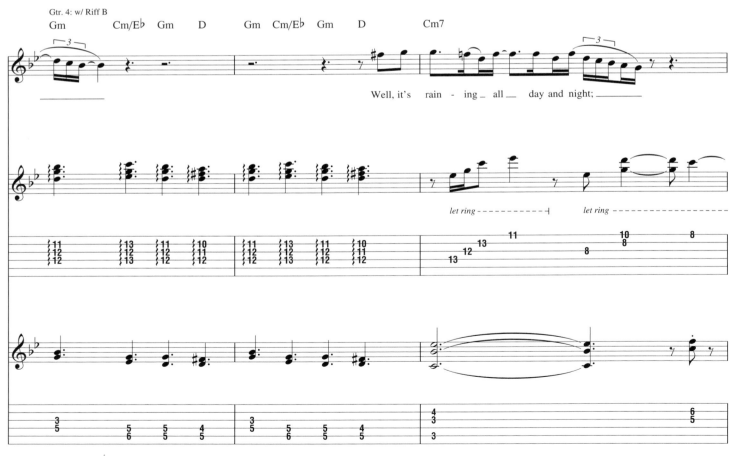

Gtr. 4: w/ Riff B

Well, it's rain - ing all day and night;

74

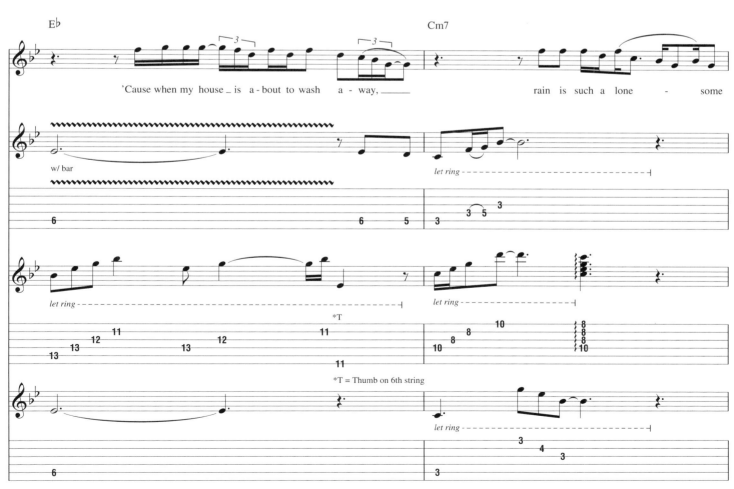

Guitar Solo

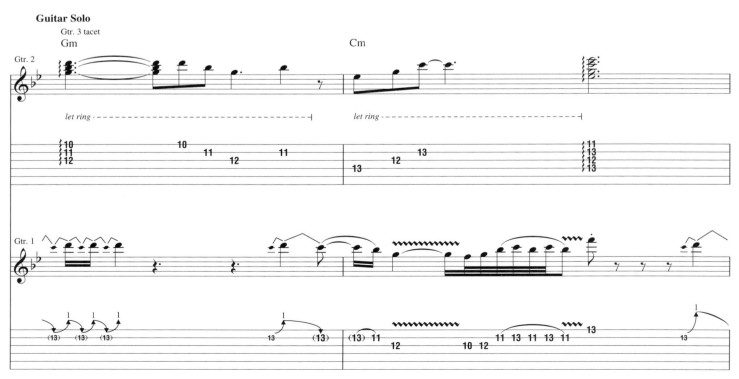

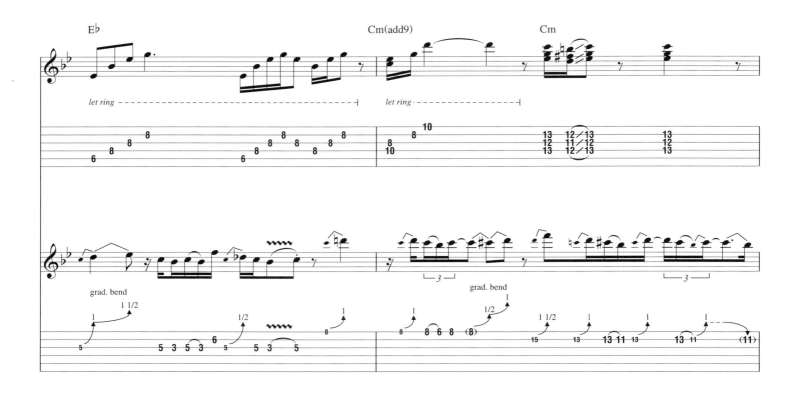

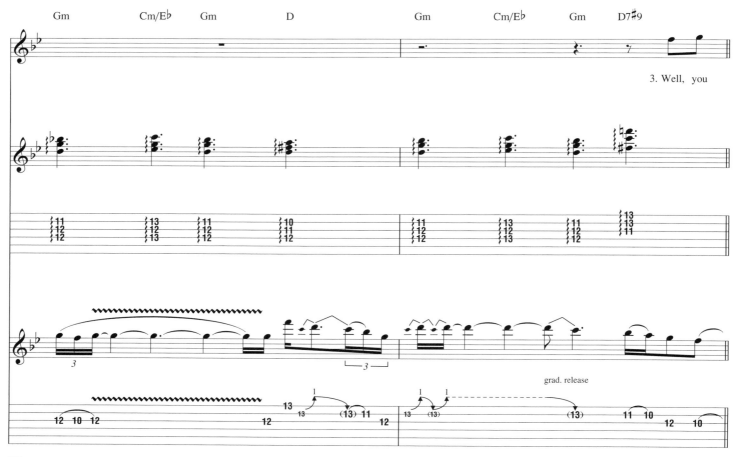

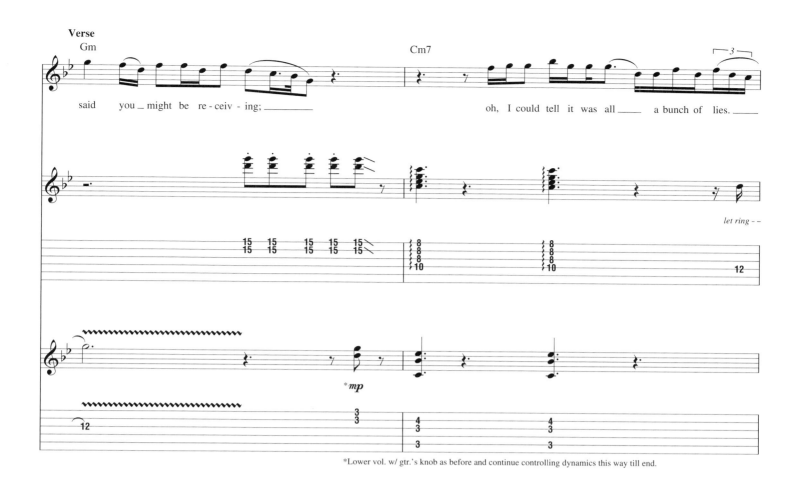

*Lower vol. w/ gtr.'s knob as before and continue controlling dynamics this way till end.

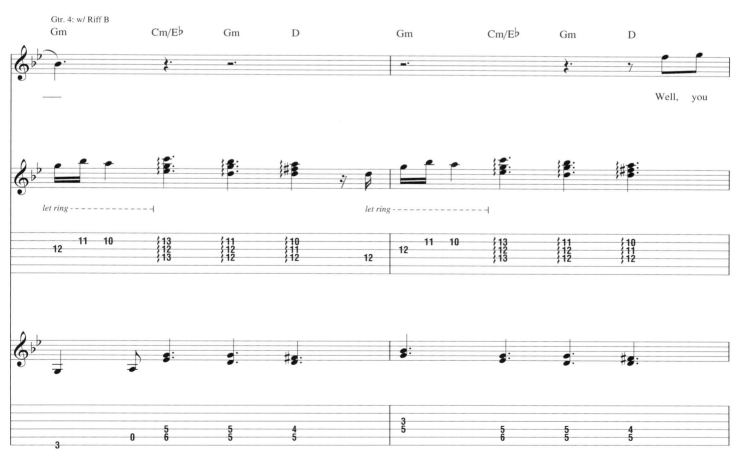

79

said you _ might _ be re - ceiv - ing; _____   oh, I could tell it was all _____ a bunch of lies. _____

let ring ------------------

let ring ------------------

let ring ------------------------

let ring ------------------------

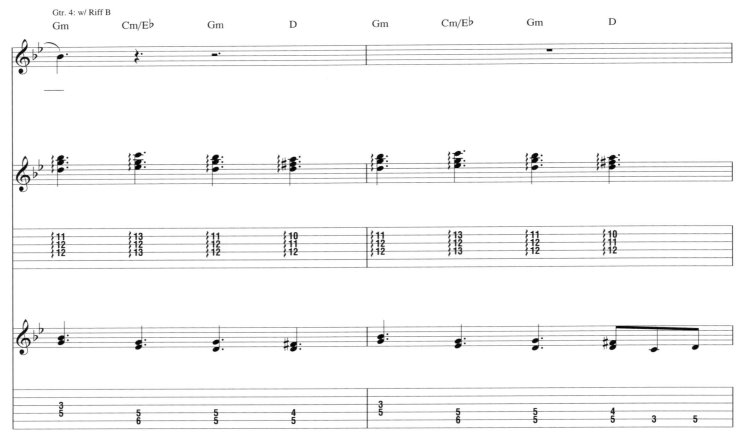

Gtr. 4: w/ Riff B

Gm   Cm/E♭   Gm   D   Gm   Cm/E♭   Gm   D

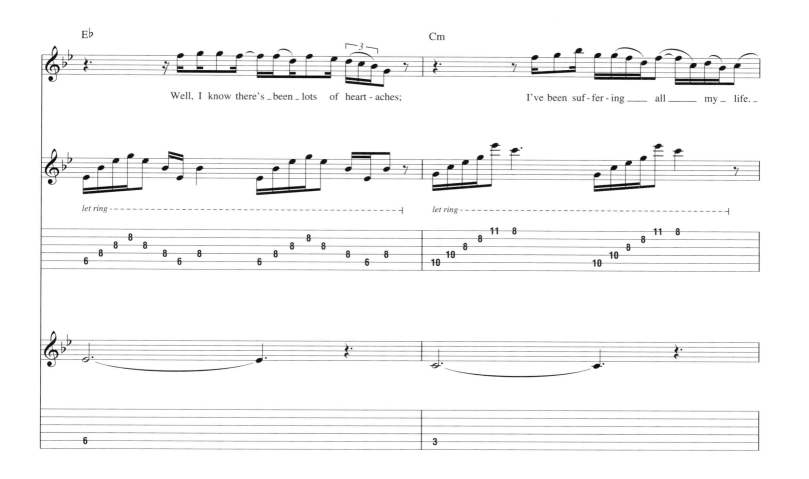

Well, I know there's _ been _ lots of heart - aches; I've been suf-fer-ing _____ all _____ my _ life. _

let ring -   *let ring -*

Gtr. 4: w/ Riff B

Suf - fer - ing. _____   Mm. _____

Rhy. Fig. 1   **End Rhy. Fig. 1**

Outro-Guitar Solo

Gtr. 2: w/ Rhy. Fig. 1 (5 times)
Gtr. 4: w/ Riff B (8 times)

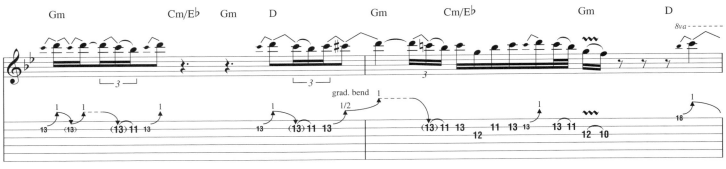

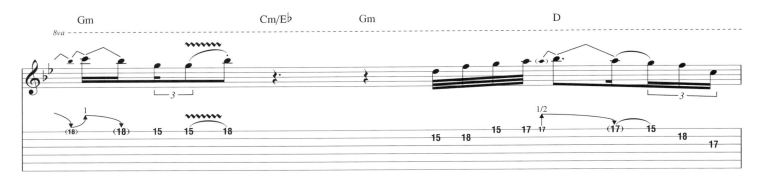

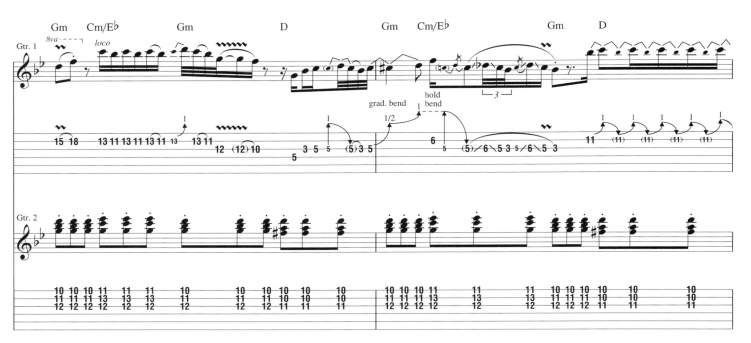

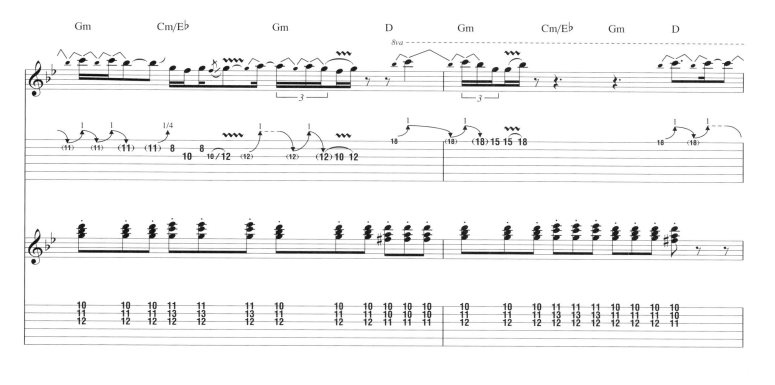

Gtr. 2: w/ Rhy. Fig. 1 (5 times)

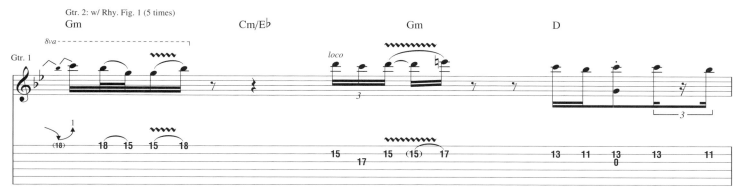

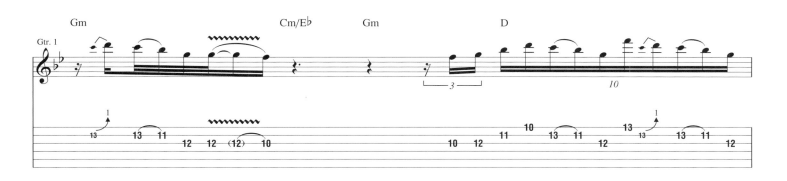

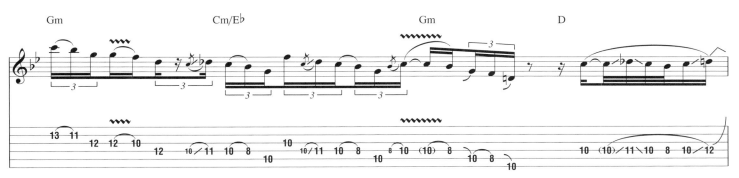

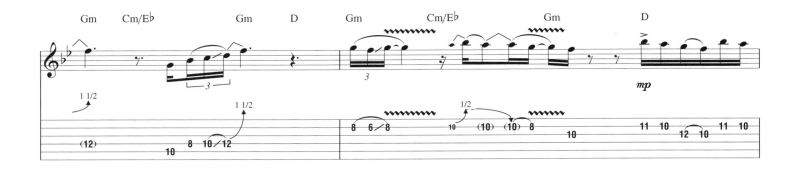

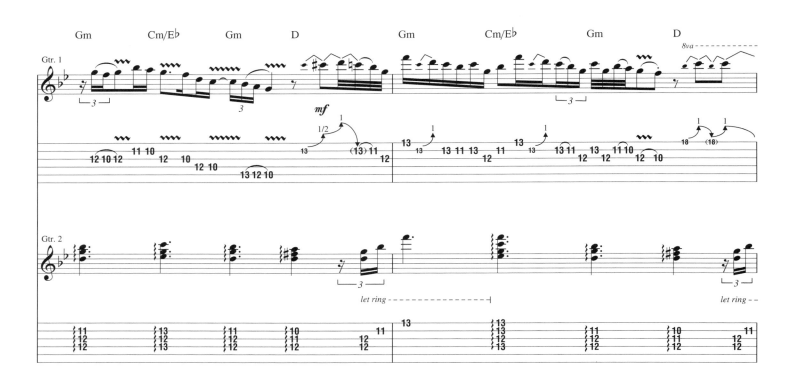

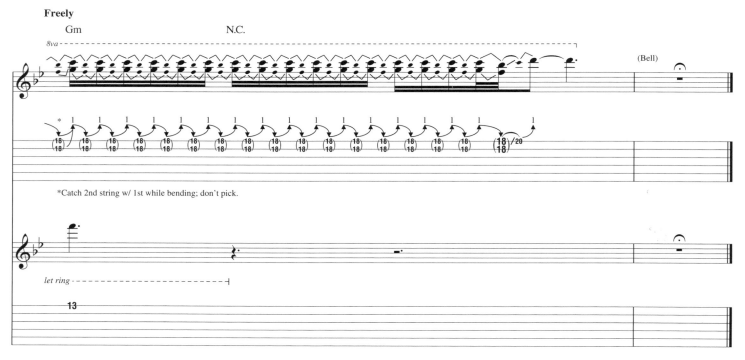

*Catch 2nd string w/ 1st while bending; don't pick.

LAST KISS

Words and Music by
Joe Bonamassa

Verse

E5

1. Tell me how high

cot - ton has to grow.

*Strum muted strings w/ thumb throughout.

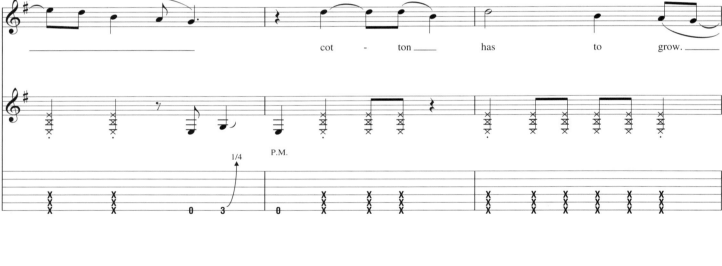

Tell me

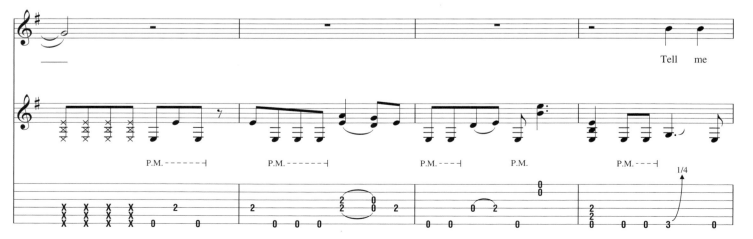

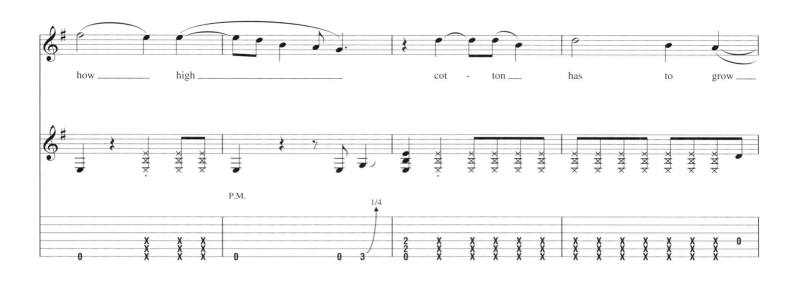

how _____ high _____ cot - ton ___ has to grow ___

P.M.

'fore you

P.M. ------| P.M. --|

E5
Rhy. Fig. 1   D5/E E5

Gtr. 2
(dist.)

f

get   a   man _____ with ___ a   rust - y   blade and a   hoe. ___

Chorus

Gtr. 2 tacet

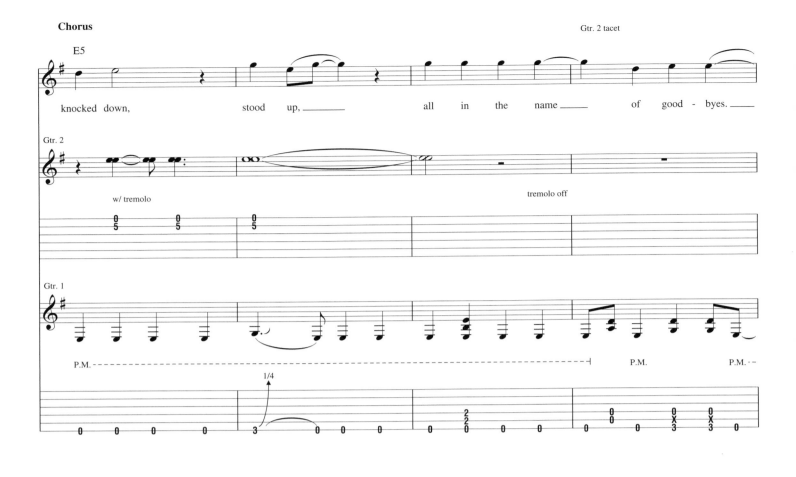

knocked down, stood up, _____ all in the name _____ of good - byes. _____

I've been

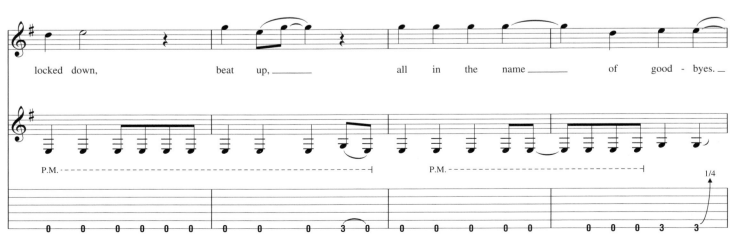

locked down, beat up, _____ all in the name _____ of good - byes. _____

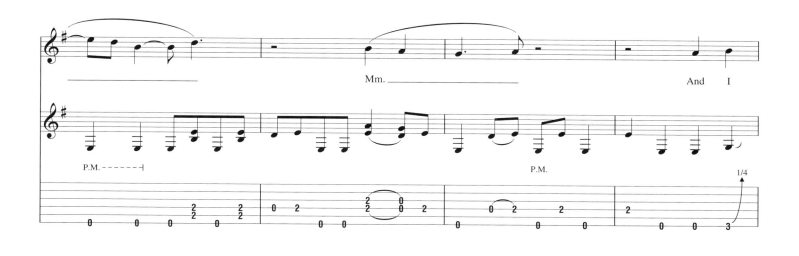

Mm. _____ And I

P.M. ----┐   P.M.   1/4

Gtr. 2: w/ Rhy. Fig. 1 (1st 4 meas.)

don't mind steal - ing the last ___ kiss be - fore ___ I die. ___

P.M. --------------------┐   1/4

E5 D5/E E5   D5/E E5   D5

Gtr. 2

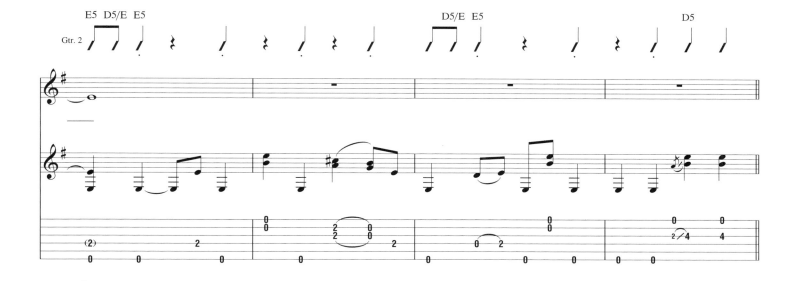

Interlude

Gtr. 2 tacet

1/4   1/2

3. Tell   me

packs his suit - case ___ and he gets ___ the hell out of town? ___

4. Now that

Gtr. 2

w/ tremolo

tremolo off

Gtr. 1

P.M. ┐   P.M.   P.M. *let ring* - ┐

Verse

Gtr. 2 tacet

E5

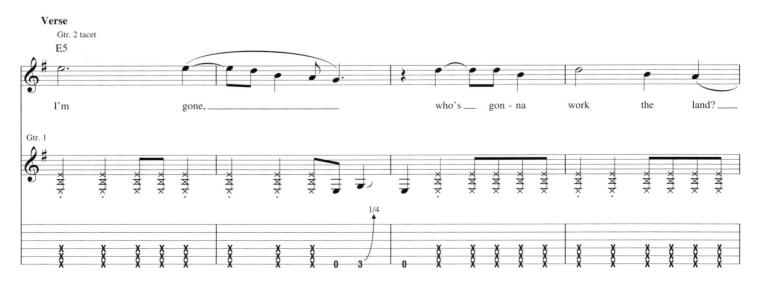

I'm gone, _____ who's ___ gon - na work the land? ___

Gtr. 1

Now that I'm _____ gone, _____ who's ___ gon-na work the land ___ just to make _____ sure _____ that ___ this dirt _____ don't turn in-to sand? ___

§ **Chorus**

Mm. _____ And I

2nd time, Gtr. 2 tacet

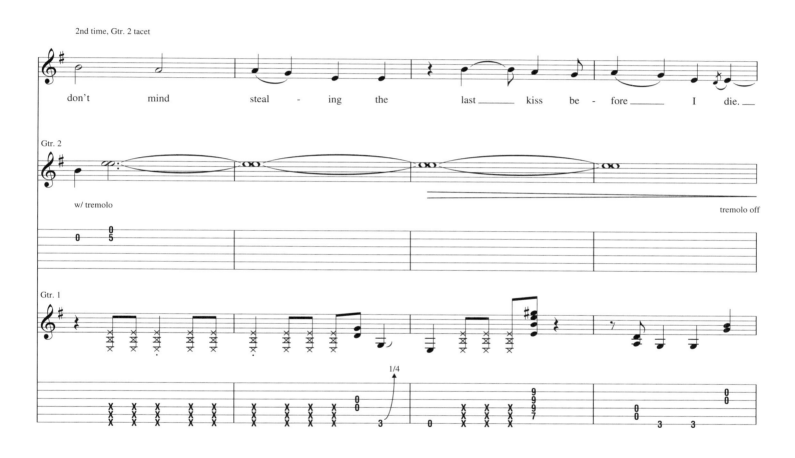

don't mind steal - ing the last _____ kiss be - fore _____ I die. _____

Gtr. 2

w/ tremolo   tremolo off

Gtr. 1

1/4

To Coda ⊕

Gtr. 2 tacet

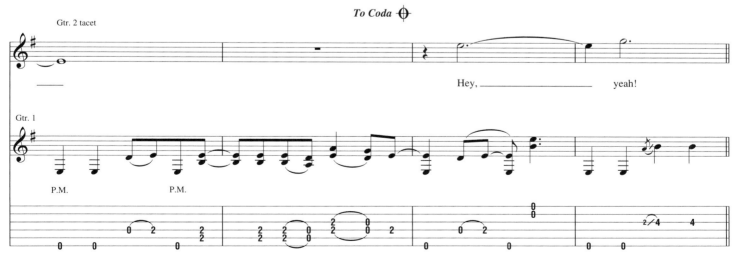

_____ Hey, _____ yeah!

Gtr. 1

P.M.   P.M.

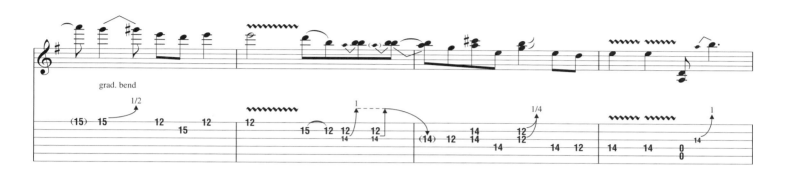

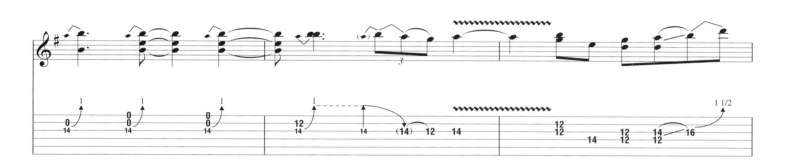

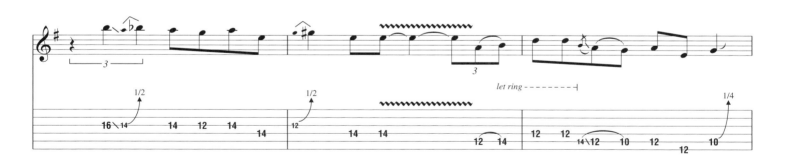

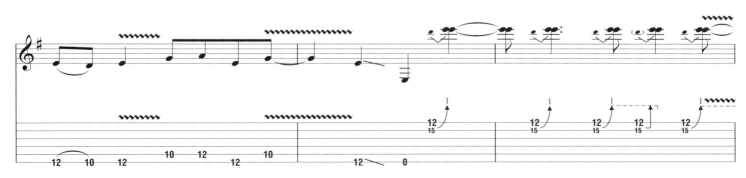

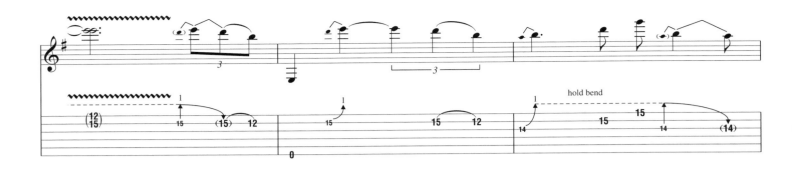

D.S. al Coda

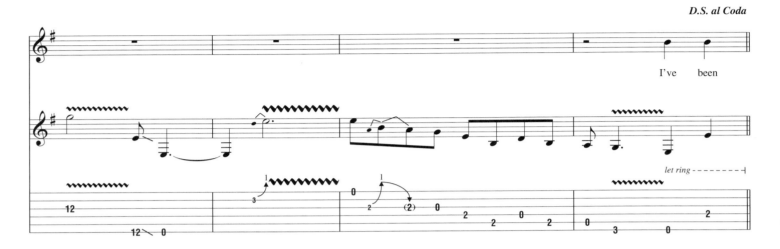

I've been

let ring - - - - - - - - -

⊕ **Coda**

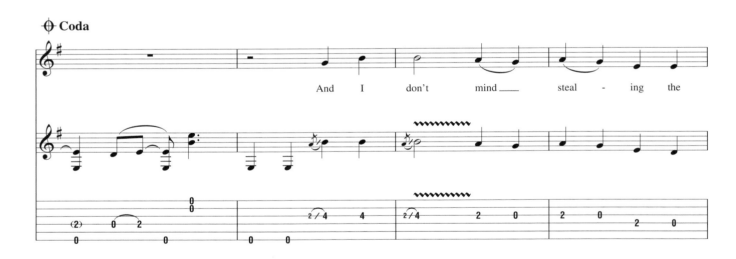

And I don't mind ___ steal - ing the

last ___ kiss be - fore ___ I die. ___ Mm,

**Gtrs. 1 & ***3

*w/ vol. knob   **Composite arrangement
                        ***Banjo arr. for gtr.

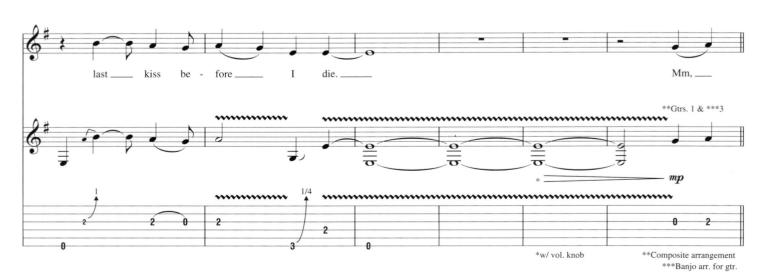

100

Outro

Gtr. 2: w/ Riff A

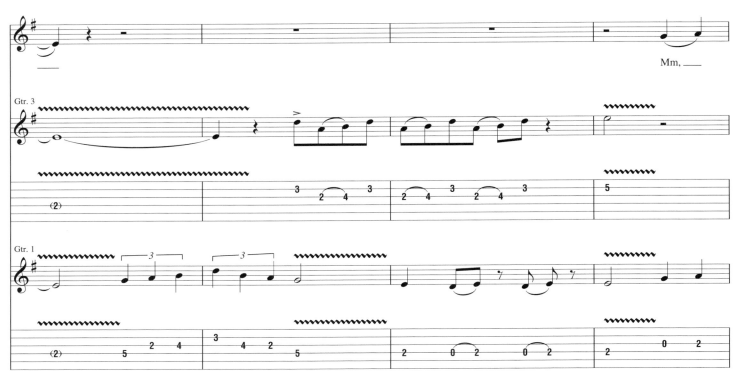

Gtr. 3 tacet

Gtr. 2: w/ Riff A

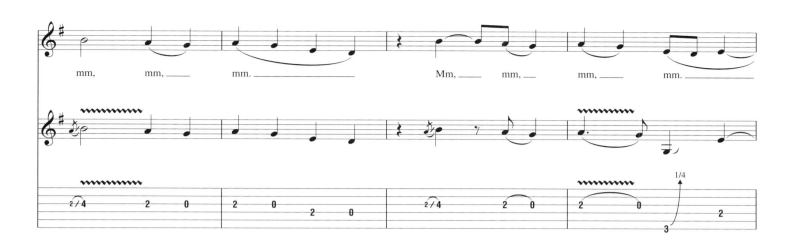

Gtr. 2: w/ Riff A

Gtr. 3 tacet

Mm, _____

Gtr. 3

Gtr. 1

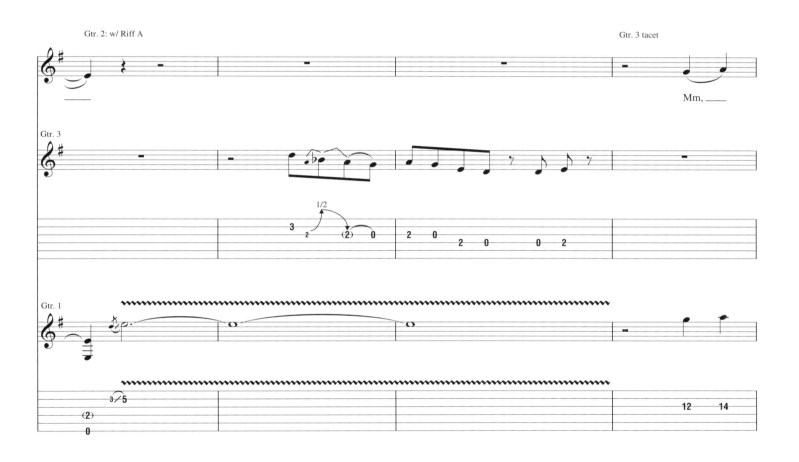

mm,   mm, _____   mm. _____   Mm, _____ mm, _____   mm, _____   mm.

Gtr. 1

grad. bend

LONESOME ROAD BLUES

Words and Music by
Joe Bonamassa

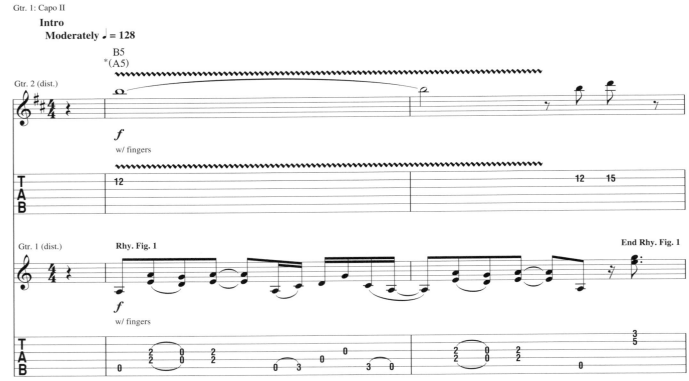

*Symbols in parentheses represent chord names respective to capoed guitar.
Symbols above reflect actual sounding chords. Capoed fret is "0" in tab.
Chord symbols reflect basic harmony.

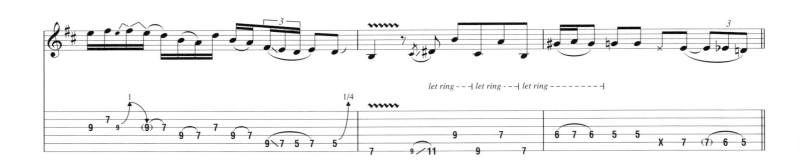

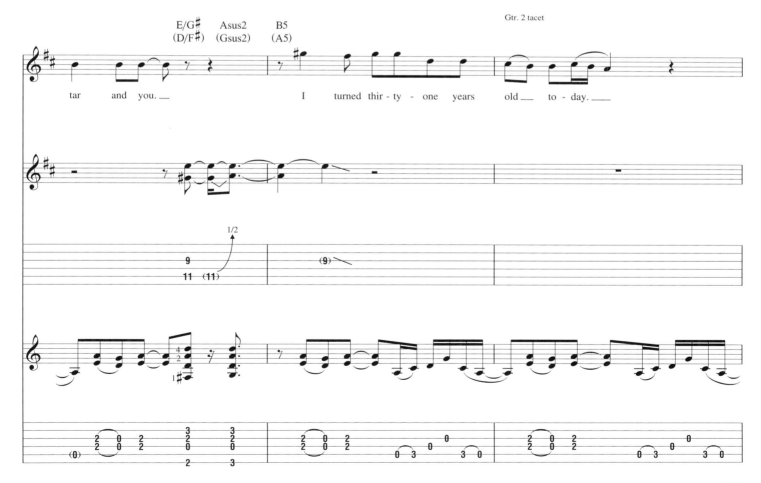

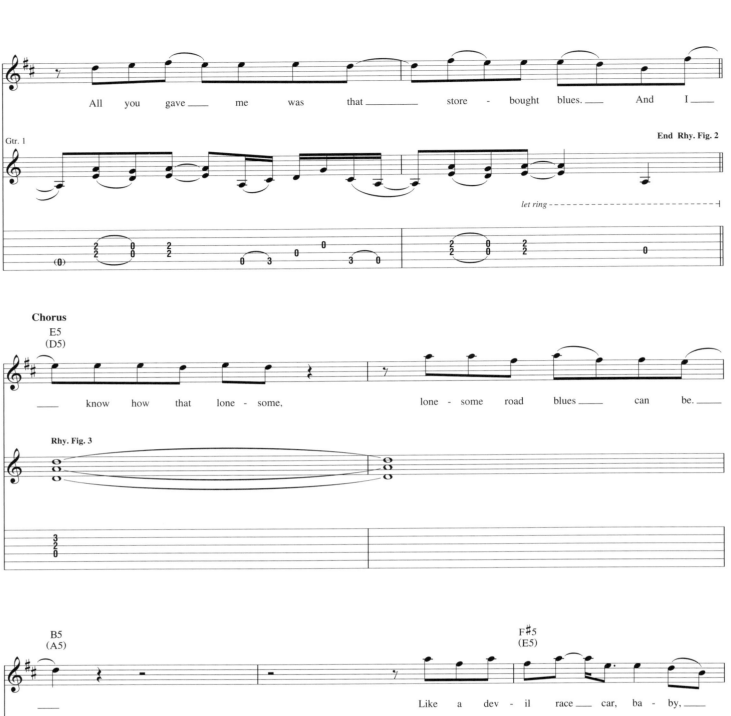

All you gave ___ me was that ___ store - bought blues. ___ And I ___

Chorus

E5
(D5)

___ know how that lone - some, lone - some road blues ___ can be. ___

B5
(A5)

F#5
(E5)

Like a dev - il race ___ car, ba - by, ___

109

Interlude

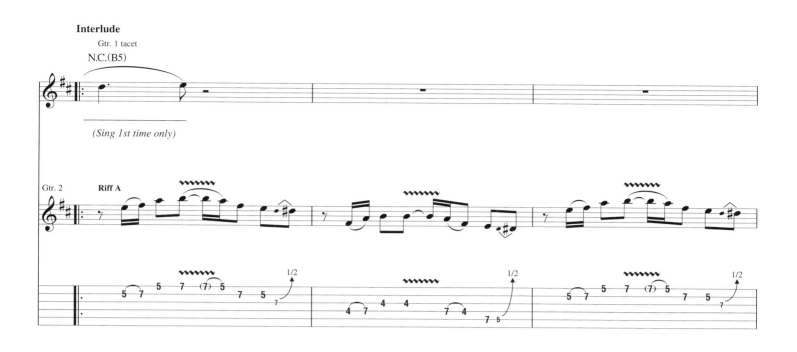

(Sing 1st time only)

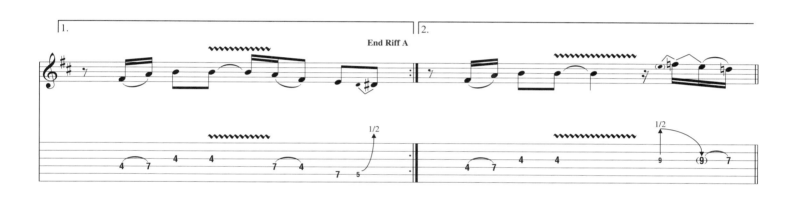

Guitar Solo

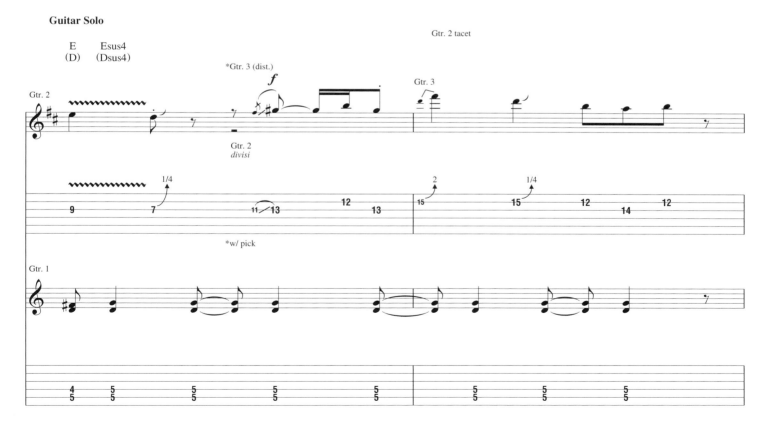

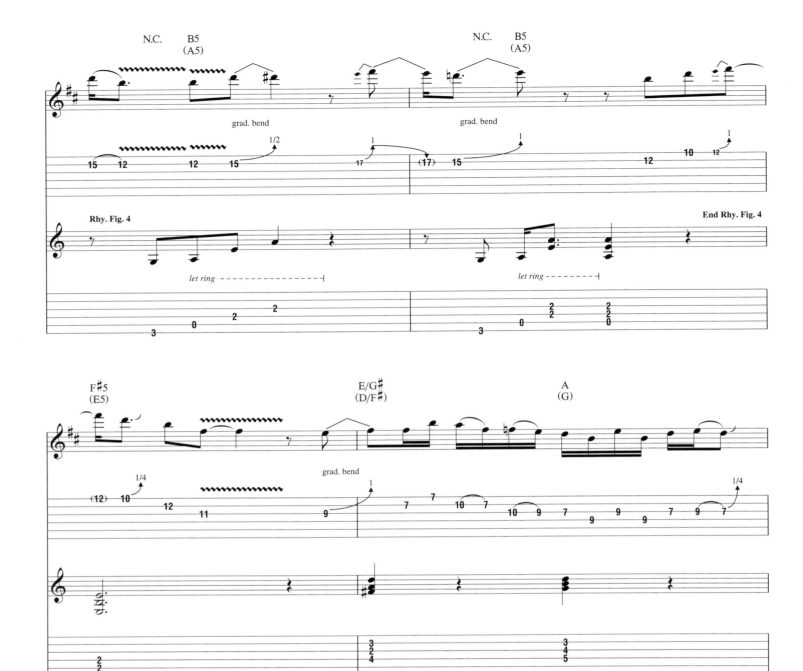

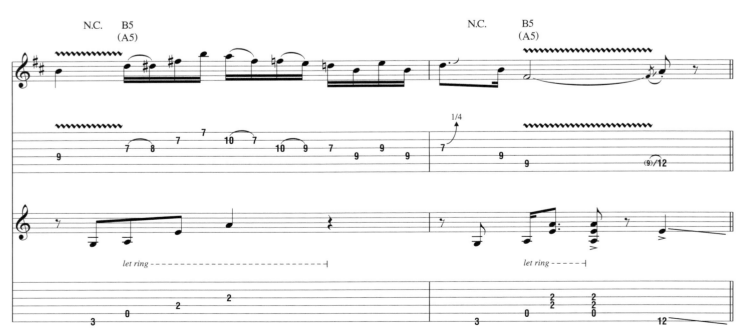

Chorus

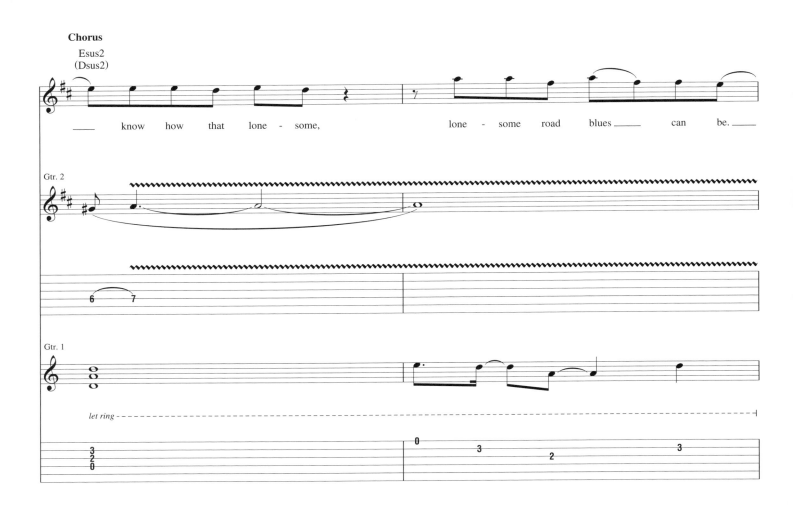

know how that lone - some, lone - some road blues ___ can be. ___

Like a dev -

114

117

ONE OF THESE DAYS

Words and Music by
Joe Bonamassa

Gtr. 1: Open E tuning:
(low to high) E-B-E-G#-B-E

Intro
Moderately slow ♩ = 67

*E5

*Chord symbols reflect basic harmony.

1. One of these days, ___

Rhy. Fig. 1

End Rhy. Fig. 1

P.M. ------- ￢

P.M.

P.M. ------- ￢

P.M. *let ring* ------- ￢

Verse

Gtr. 1 tacet
*Gtrs. 2 & 3: w/ Rhy. Fig. 1 (4 times)

E5

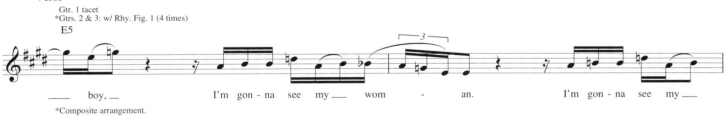

___ boy, ___ I'm gon - na see my ___ wom - an. I'm gon - na see my ___

*Composite arrangement.

chil - dren, the chil - dren on my ___ knee. ___ Gon - na run up to my

Gtr. 1

P.M.   P.M.

wom - an ____ and hold her in my ___ arms. ____ With tears ___ in her

eyes _____ she says, "I'm glad you're _____ free." ____

Interlude

E5

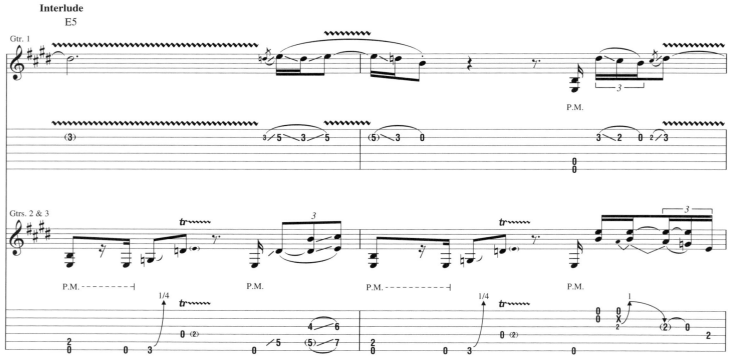

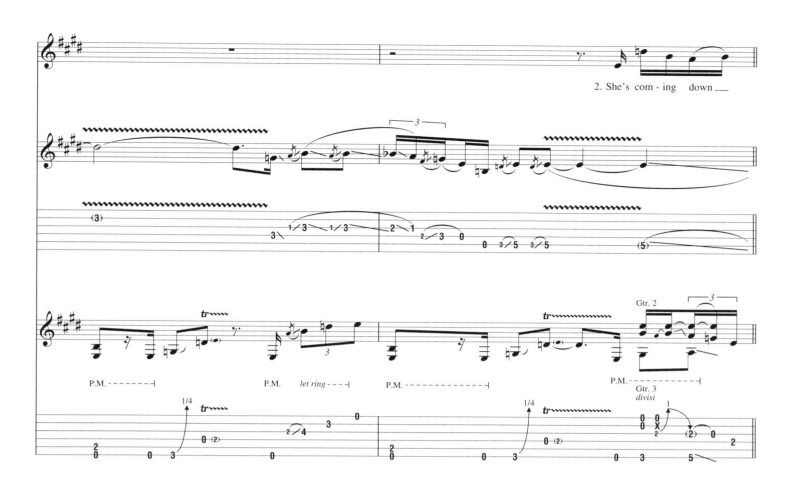

2. She's com - ing down ___

Verse

Gtr. 3: w/ Rhy. Fig. 1 (3 1/2 times)

E5

the road, ___ boy. I said she's com - ing down ___ the road. ___ She's got a red dress on. ___

Gtr. 2: w/ Rhy. Fig. 2 (2 times)

Yeah, she's got a red dress on. _____ She's com-ing down the

*Played as even 16th notes.

road, boy, _____ with her bags _ down low. _____ Said she com-ing down the

road, boy. _____ She's got her bags down _ low. _____ Hey, _ yeah.

122

Interlude

Gtr. 2: w/ Rhy. Fig. 2 (2 times)

Verse

Gtrs. 2 & 3: w/ Rhy. Fig. 1 (2 times)

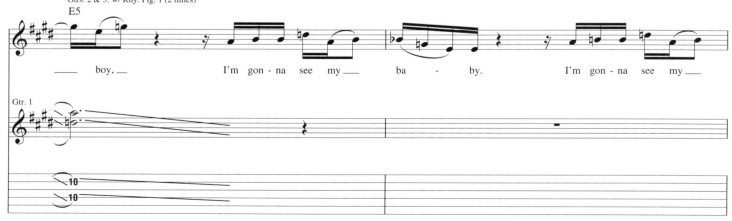

——— boy, ——— I'm gon-na see my ——— ba - by. I'm gon-na see my ———

ba - by.   I'm com - ing down the road._____   Gon - na have my par -

*Played as even 16th notes.

Gtr. 3: w/ Rhy. Fig. 1 (1st meas.)   Gtr. 2: w/ Rhy. Fig. 1 (last meas.)

don, __   par - don in her __ a - pron, lord, lord. __   Want to see the

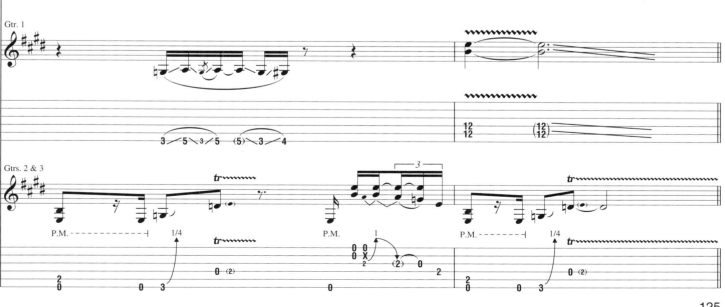

gov - er - nor. _____   She said, "Re - lease my _____ man."   Hey. _____

125

126

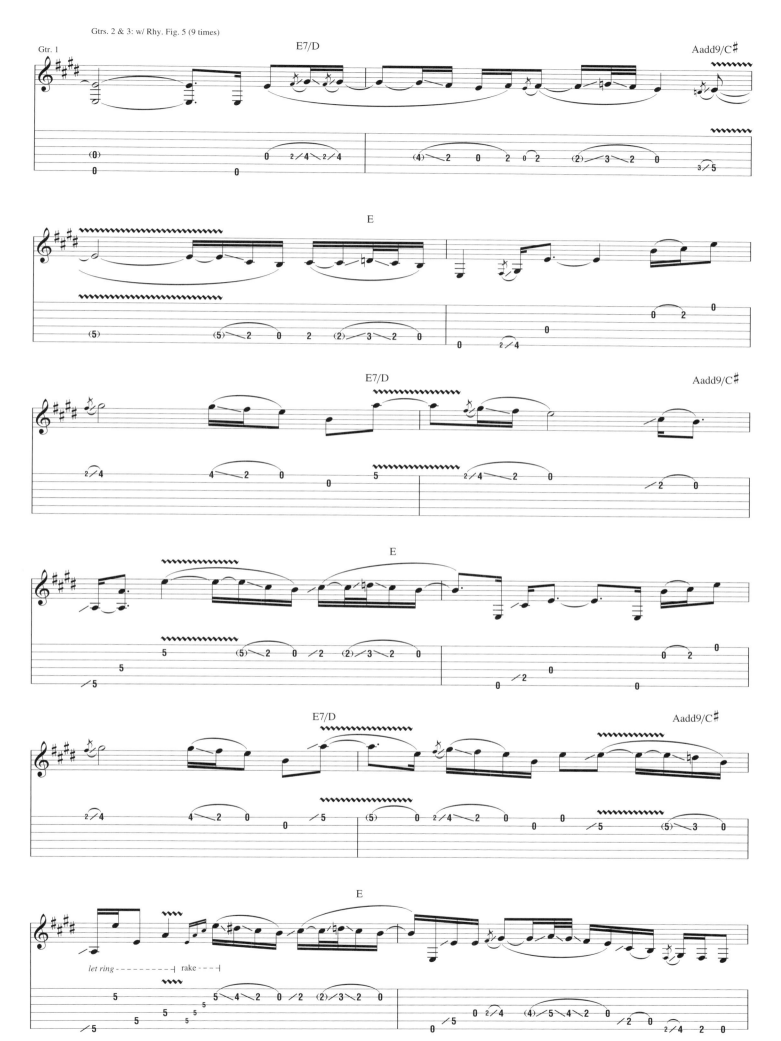

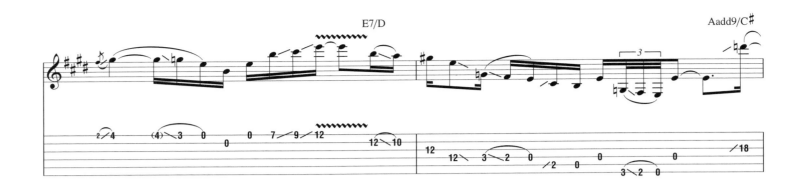

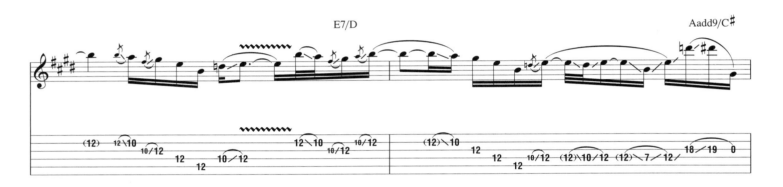

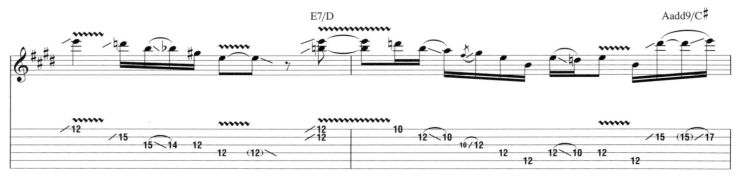

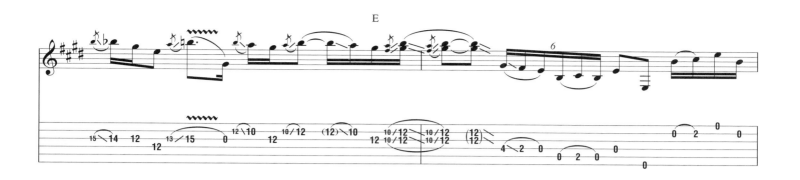

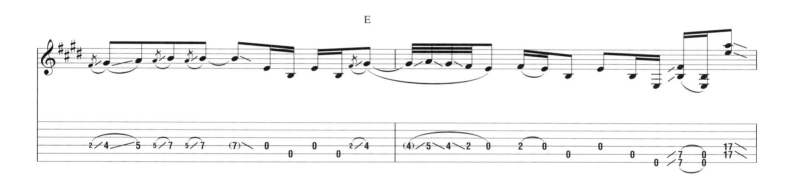

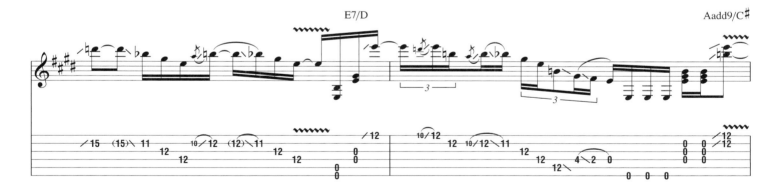

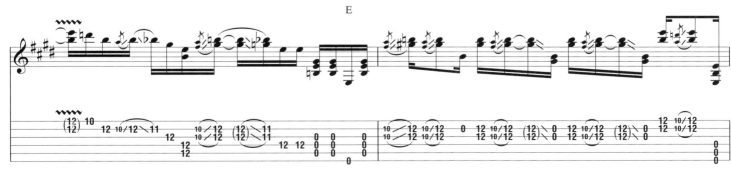

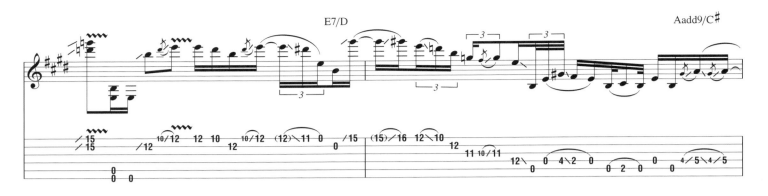

E7/D   Aadd9/C#

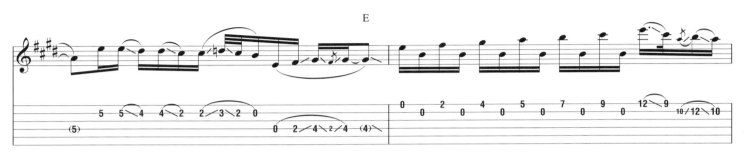

E

E7   Aadd9

Gtr. 1

Gtrs. 2 & 3

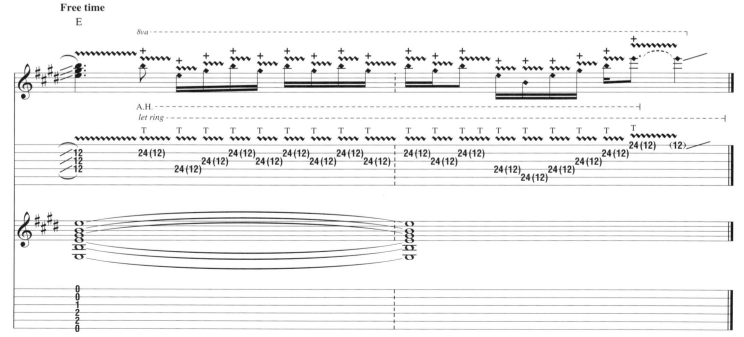

Free time

E

SLOE GIN

Words and Music by
Bob Ezrin and Michael Kamen

131

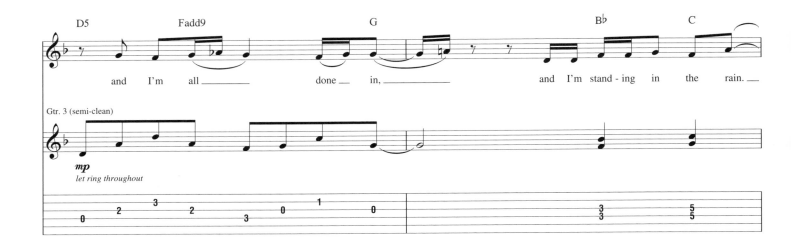

and I'm all _____ done _____ in, _____ and I'm stand - ing in the rain. _____

Gtr. 3 (semi-clean)

mp
let ring throughout

_____ And I feel _____ like I'm gon - na cry. _____

Chorus

I'm so damn lone - ly, and I ain't e - ven high. _____

Rhy. Fig. 2A
Gtr. 4 (semi-clean)

mf
let ring throughout

Gtr. 3 **Rhy. Fig. 2**

mf

*Using a guitar with Les Paul style electronics, set lead volume to 10 and rhythm volume to 0. Strike the strings while the pickup selector switch is in the lead position, then flip the switch in the rhythm indicated to simulate the re-attack.

Lyrics:
storm - y seas. ___ Well, I feel ___ like I'm drift - ing ___ a - way. ___ Can't ___ seem to get a grip on me, ___ and I can't ___ e - ven try. ___

Chorus
Gtrs. 3 & 4: w/ Rhy. Figs. 2 & 2A

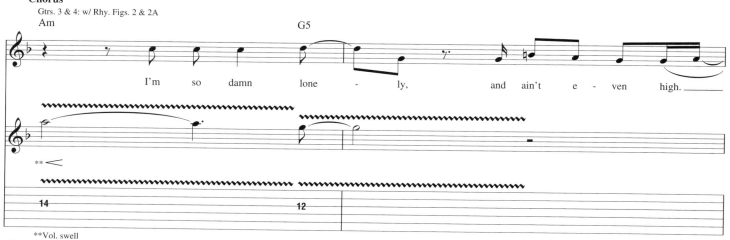

I'm so damn lone - ly, and ain't e - ven high. ___

**Vol. swell

Guitar Solo
Gtr. 1: w/ Rhy. Fig. 1 (8 times)
Gtrs. 3 & 4 tacet

I'm so damn lone - ly.

Outro-Guitar Solo

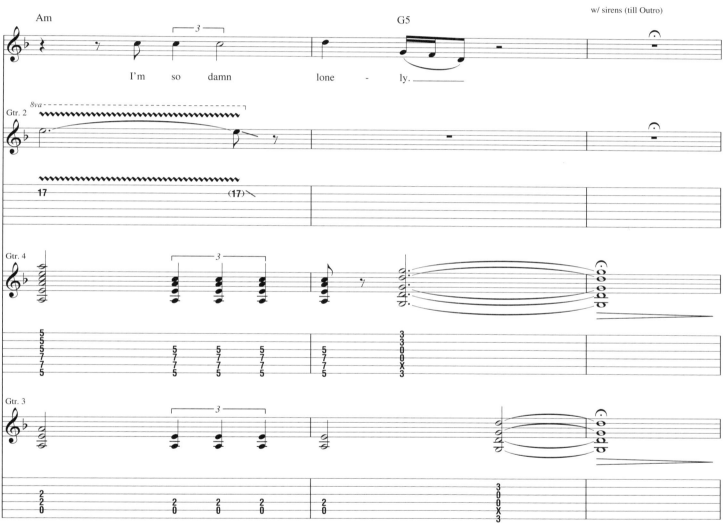

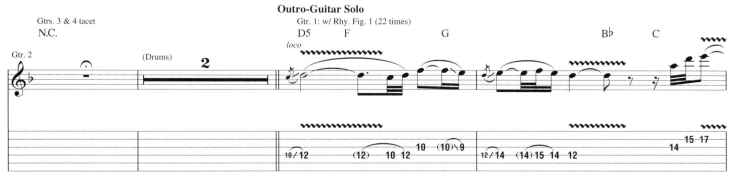

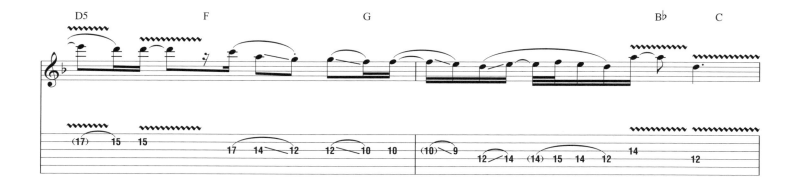

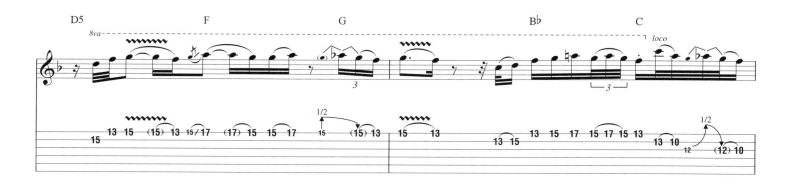

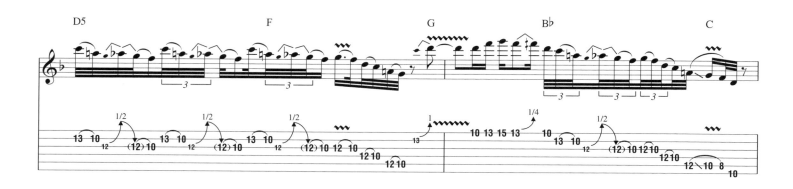

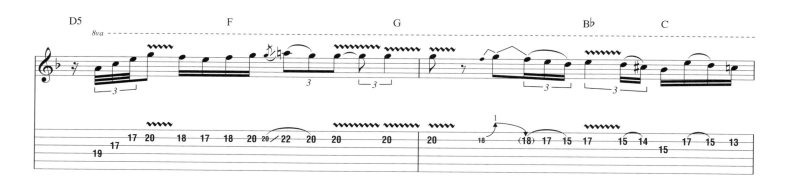

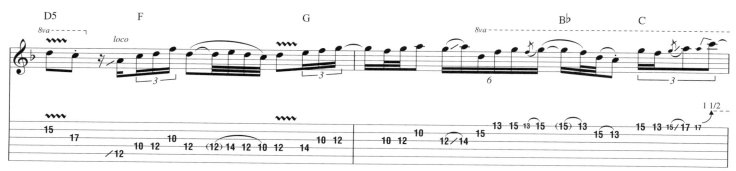

140

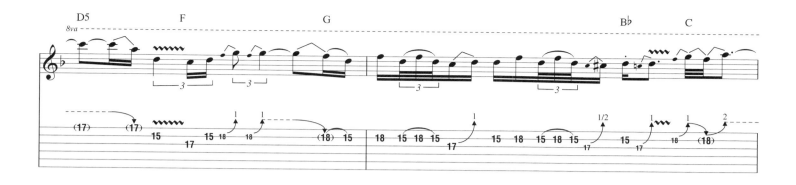

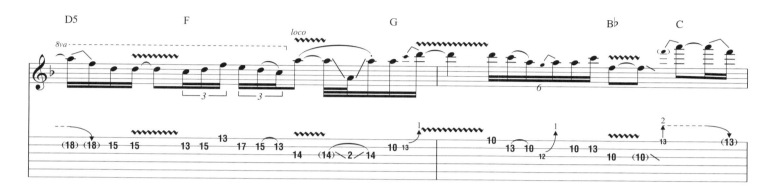

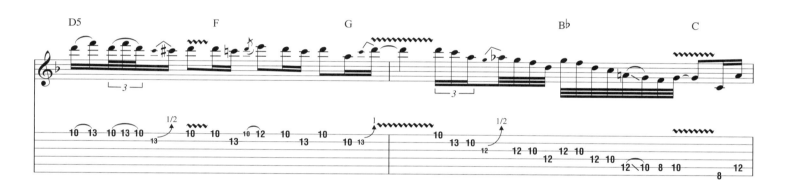

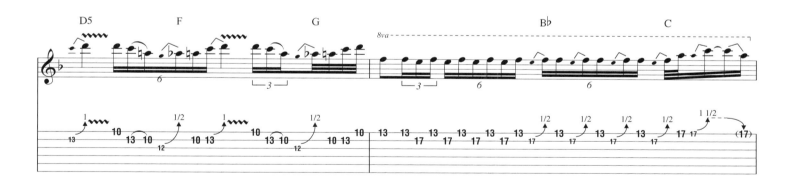

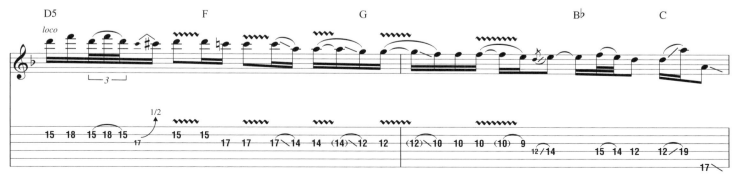

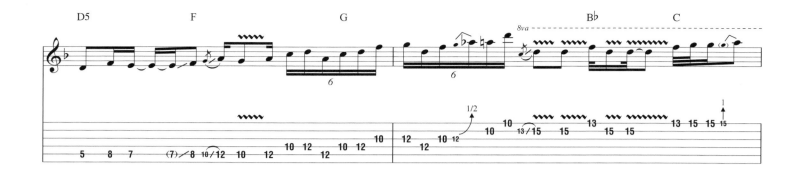

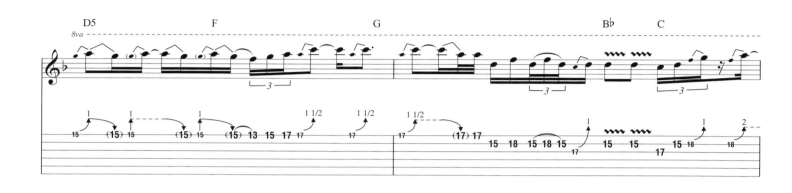

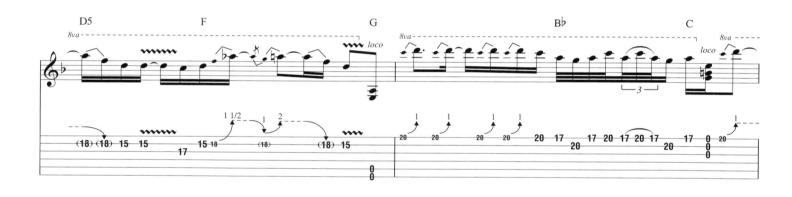

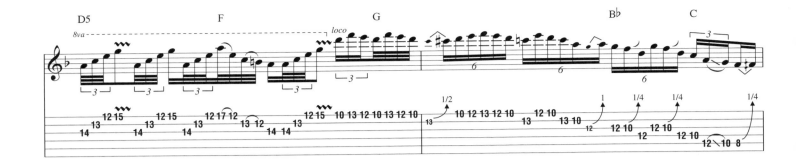

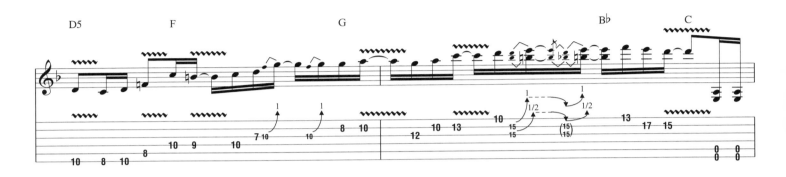

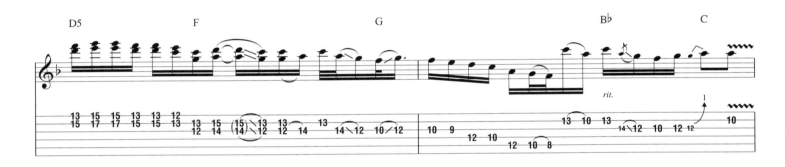

Free time

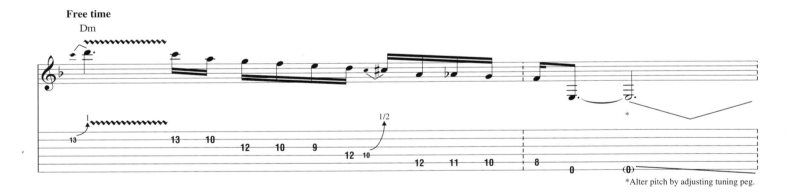

*Alter pitch by adjusting tuning peg.

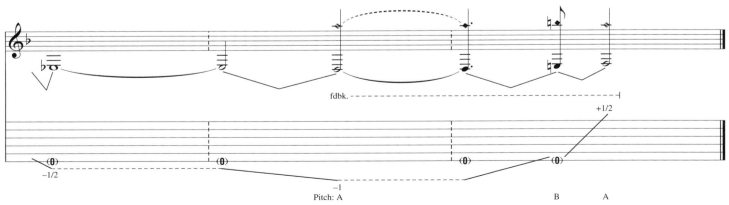

SO MANY ROADS, SO MANY TRAINS

Words and Music by
Paul Marshall

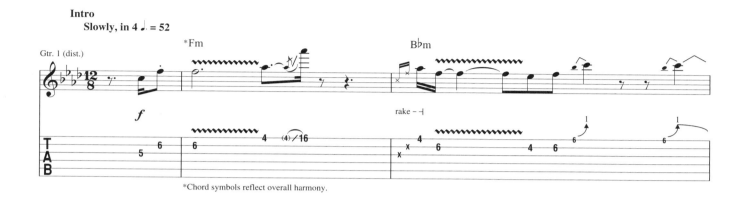

*Chord symbols reflect overall harmony.

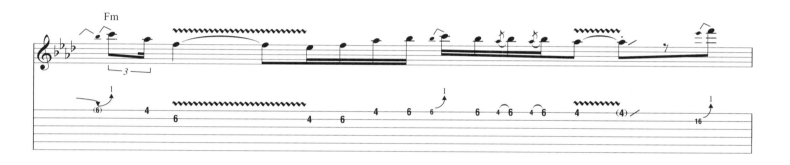

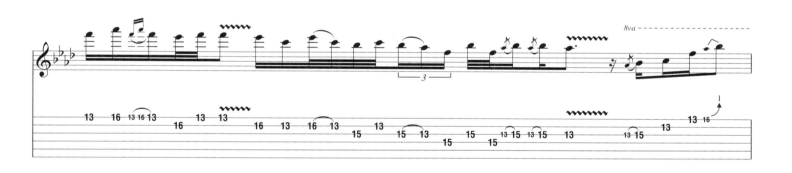

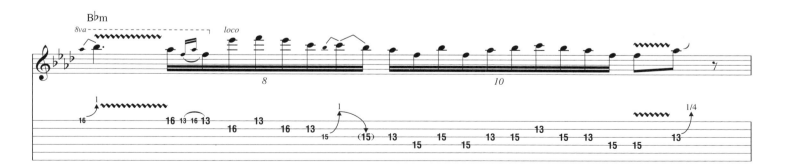

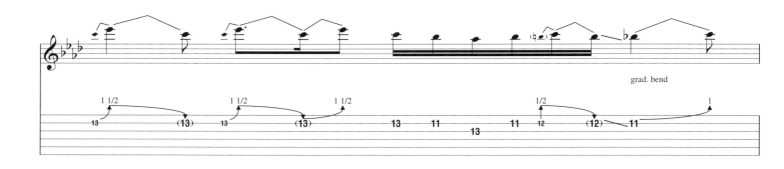

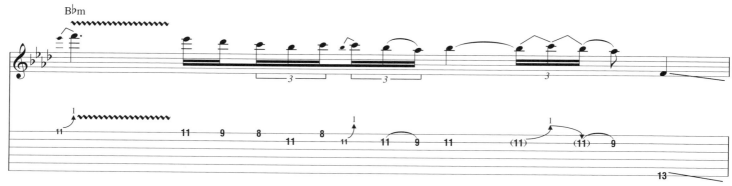

Verse

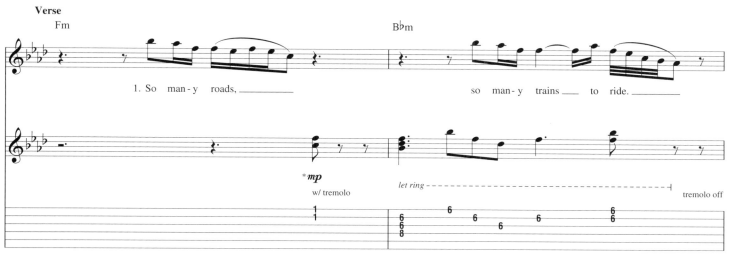

1. So man-y roads, _____ so man-y trains ___ to ride. ___

mp
w/ tremolo

let ring - tremolo off

*Lower vol. w/ gtr.'s knob, thereby decreasing dist. level.

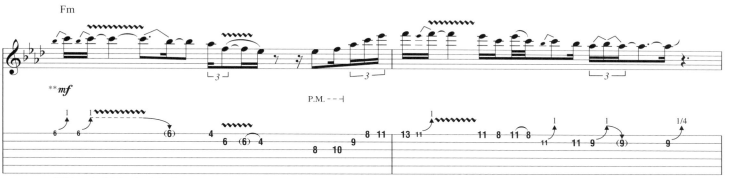

**mf*
P.M. - - -

**Raise vol. slightly w/ gtr.'s knob.

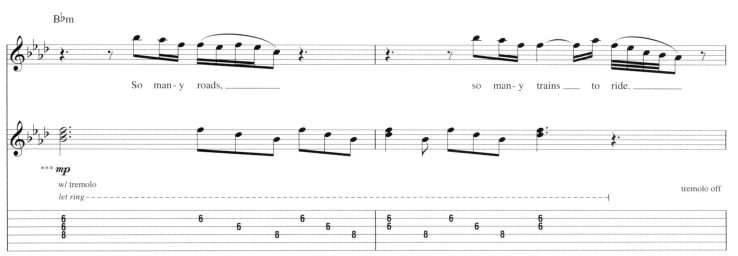

So man-y roads, _____ so man-y trains ___ to ride. ___

***mp*
w/ tremolo
let ring - tremolo off

***Continue controlling dynamics w/ gtr.'s vol. knob till end (unless otherwise indicated).

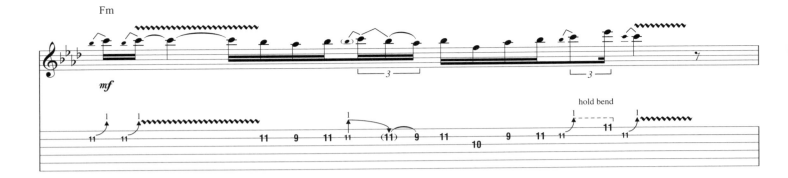

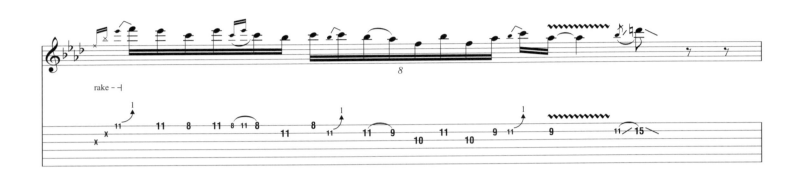

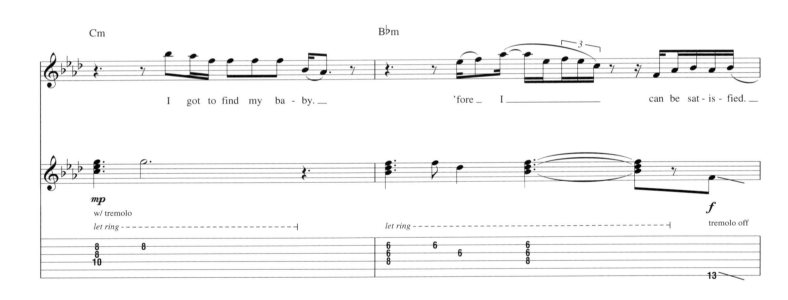

I got to find my ba - by. __

'fore __ I _____

can be sat - is - fied. __

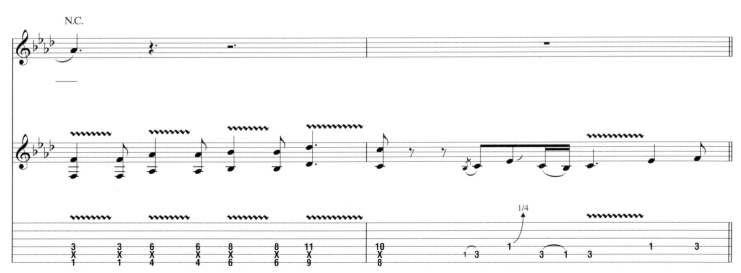

Verse

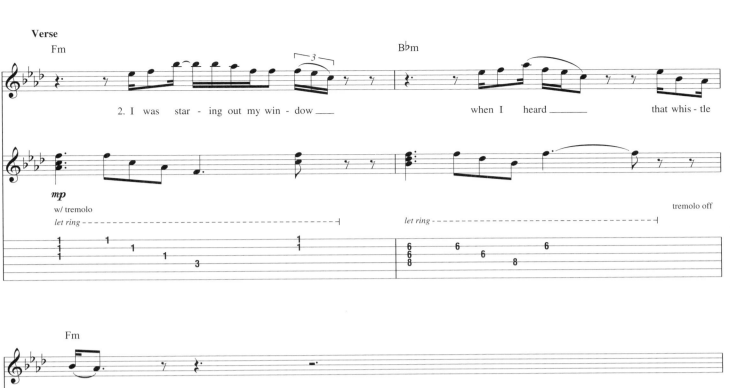

2. I was star - ing out my win - dow _____ when I heard _____ that whis - tle

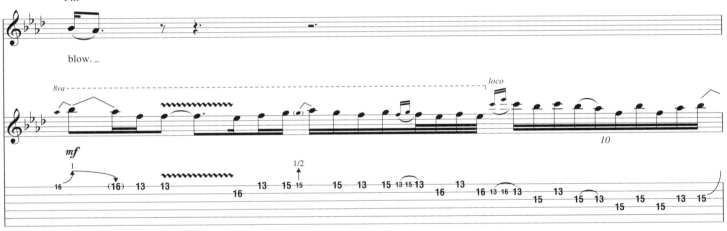

blow. _

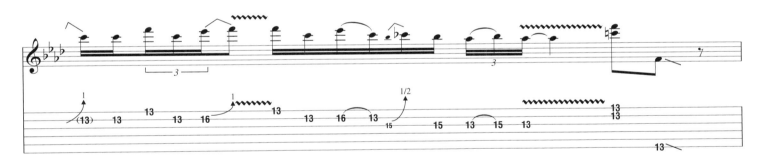

I was star - ing out my win - dow _____ when I heard _____ that whis - tle

149

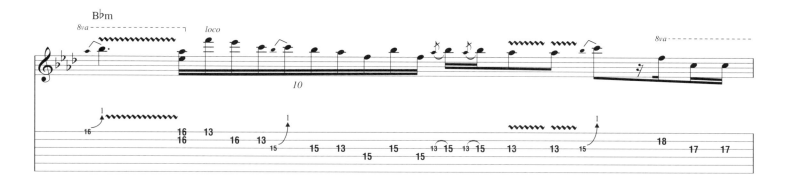

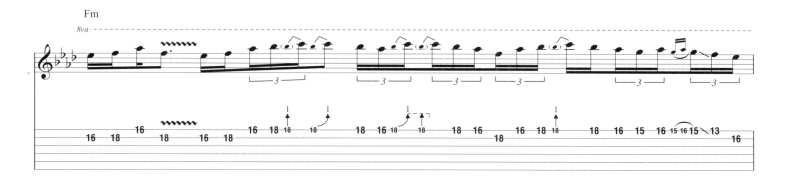

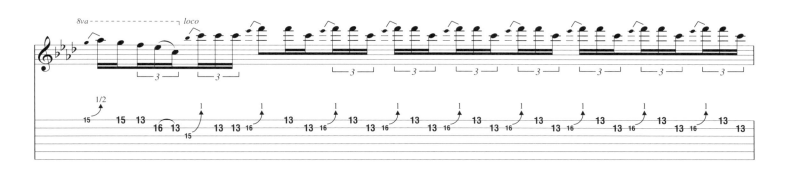

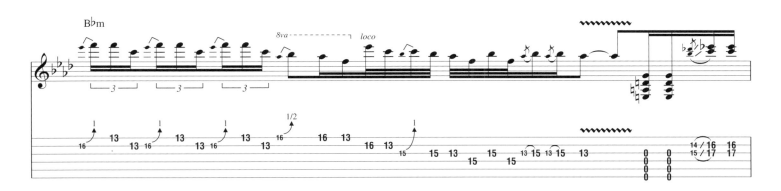

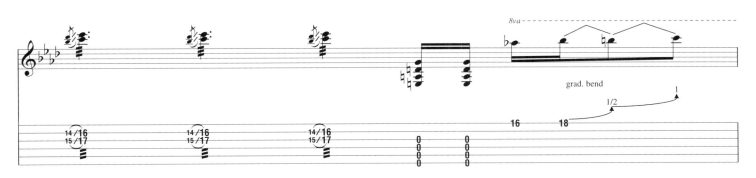

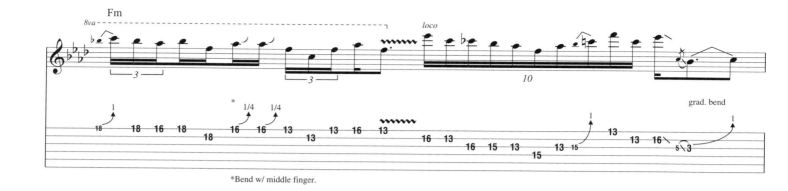

*Bend w/ middle finger.

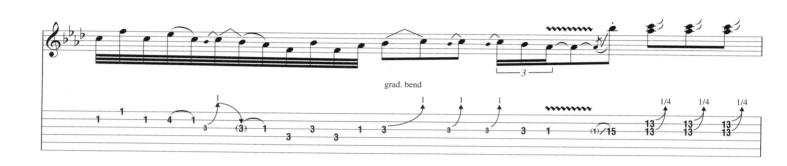

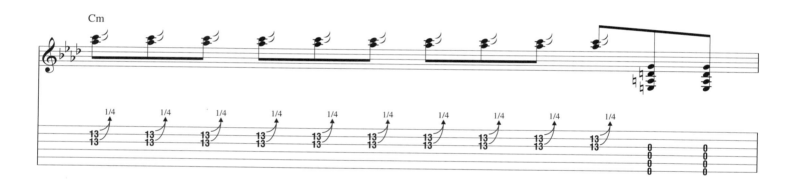

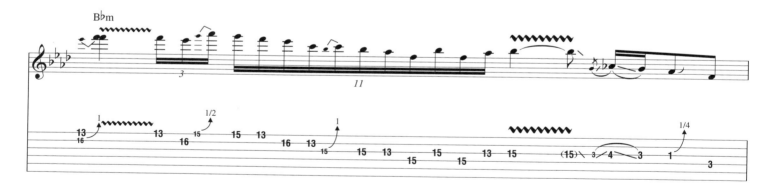

Verse

3. It was a mean old fire-man and a cruel en - gin - eer.

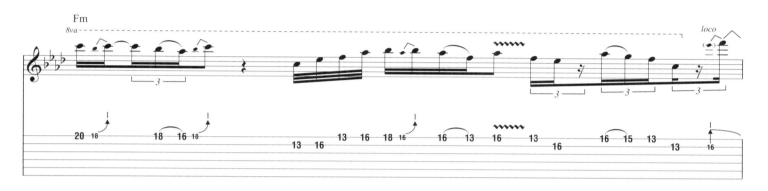

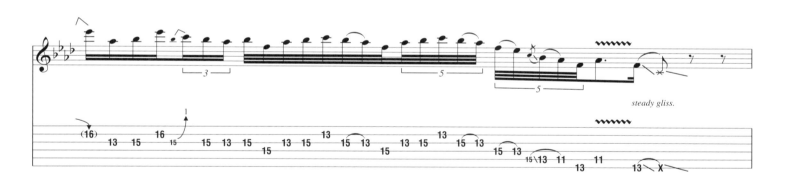

It was a mean old fire-man and a cruel en - gin - eer.

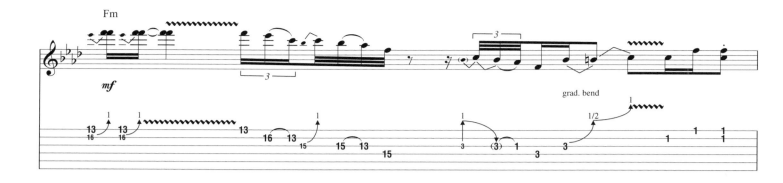

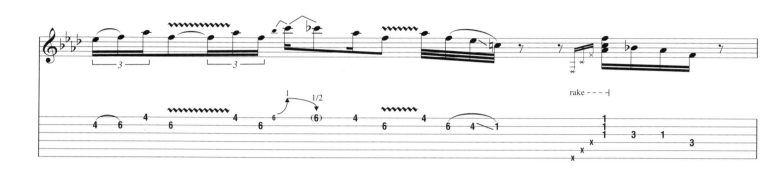

Yes, they took my ba - by, yeah, ___ oh, ___ and left me ___ stand - ing here. ___

*Bend w/ middle finger.

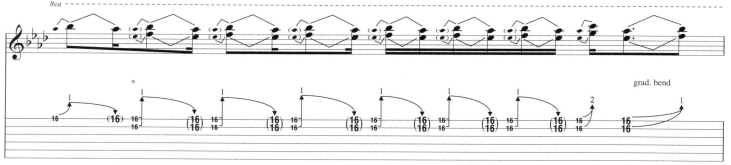

*Catch and bend both strings w/ ring finger.

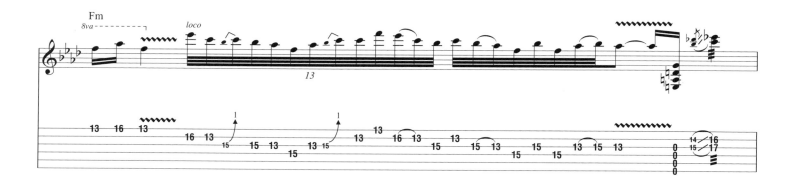

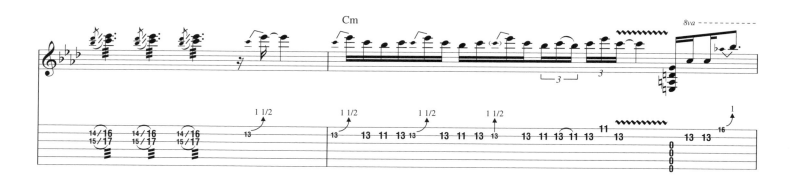

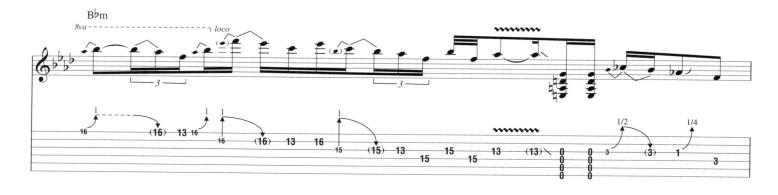

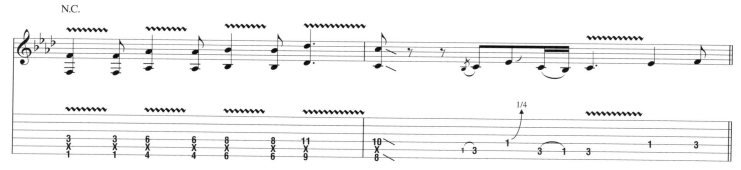

Verse

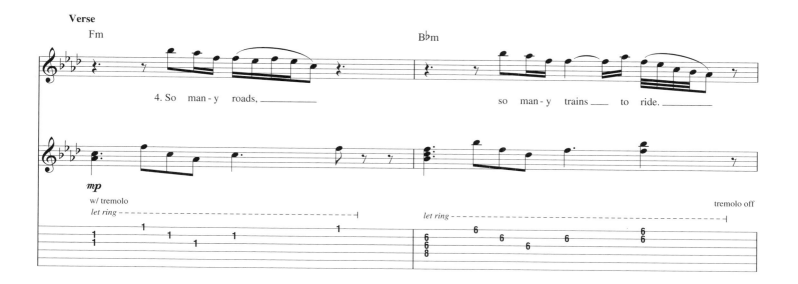

4. So man-y roads, _____ so man-y trains _____ to ride. _____

mp
w/ tremolo
let ring - - - - - - - - - - - - - - - - - - tremolo off
let ring - - - - - - - - - - - - - - - - - -

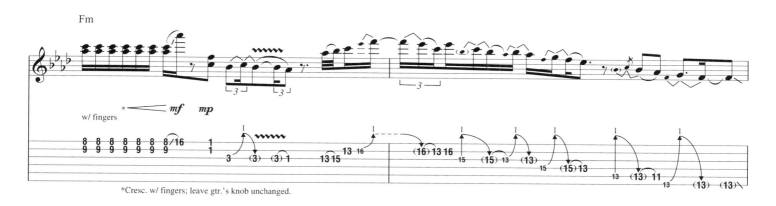

w/ fingers *mf* *mp*

*Cresc. w/ fingers; leave gtr.'s knob unchanged.

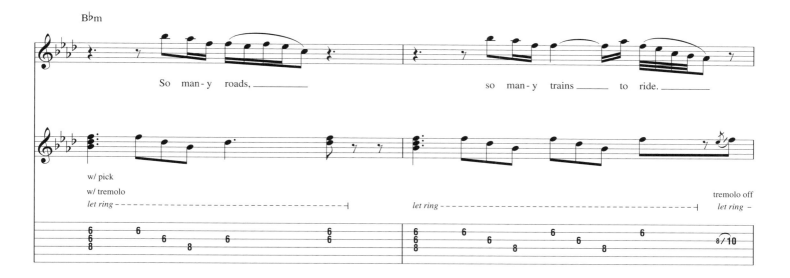

So man-y roads, _____ so man-y trains _____ to ride. _____

w/ pick
w/ tremolo
let ring - - - - - - - - - - - - - - - - - - tremolo off
let ring - - - - - - - - - - - - - - - - - - *let ring* -

mf
let ring - - - - - - -

I got to find my ba - by __ 'fore __ I'm __ sat - is - fied. __

Yeah. __ Mm. __

GUITAR NOTATION LEGEND

Guitar music can be notated three different ways: on a *musical staff*, in *tablature*, and in *rhythm slashes*.

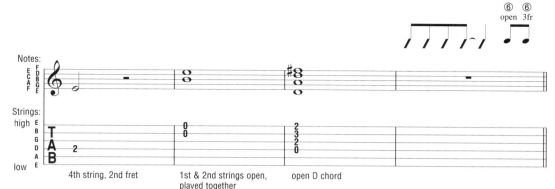

RHYTHM SLASHES are written above the staff. Strum chords in the rhythm indicated. Use the chord diagrams found at the top of the first page of the transcription for the appropriate chord voicings. Round noteheads indicate single notes.

THE MUSICAL STAFF shows pitches and rhythms and is divided by bar lines into measures. Pitches are named after the first seven letters of the alphabet.

TABLATURE graphically represents the guitar fingerboard. Each horizontal line represents a string, and each number represents a fret.

HALF-STEP BEND: Strike the note and bend up 1/2 step.

BEND AND RELEASE: Strike the note and bend up as indicated, then release back to the original note. Only the first note is struck.

HAMMER-ON: Strike the first (lower) note with one finger, then sound the higher note (on the same string) with another finger by fretting it without picking.

TRILL: Very rapidly alternate between the notes indicated by continuously hammering on and pulling off.

PICK SCRAPE: The edge of the pick is rubbed down (or up) the string, producing a scratchy sound.

TREMOLO PICKING: The note is picked as rapidly and continuously as possible.

WHOLE-STEP BEND: Strike the note and bend up one step.

PRE-BEND: Bend the note as indicated, then strike it.

PULL-OFF: Place both fingers on the notes to be sounded. Strike the first note and without picking, pull the finger off to sound the second (lower) note.

TAPPING: Hammer ("tap") the fret indicated with the pick-hand index or middle finger and pull off to the note fretted by the fret hand.

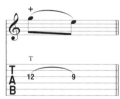

MUFFLED STRINGS: A percussive sound is produced by laying the fret hand across the string(s) without depressing, and striking them with the pick hand.

VIBRATO BAR DIVE AND RETURN: The pitch of the note or chord is dropped a specified number of steps (in rhythm), then returned to the original pitch.

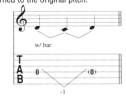

GRACE NOTE BEND: Strike the note and immediately bend up as indicated.

VIBRATO: The string is vibrated by rapidly bending and releasing the note with the fretting hand.

LEGATO SLIDE: Strike the first note and then slide the same fret-hand finger up or down to the second note. The second note is not struck.

NATURAL HARMONIC: Strike the note while the fret-hand lightly touches the string directly over the fret indicated.

PALM MUTING: The note is partially muted by the pick hand lightly touching the string(s) just before the bridge.

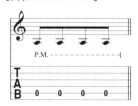

VIBRATO BAR SCOOP: Depress the bar just before striking the note, then quickly release the bar.

SLIGHT (MICROTONE) BEND: Strike the note and bend up 1/4 step.

WIDE VIBRATO: The pitch is varied to a greater degree by vibrating with the fretting hand.

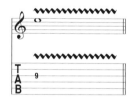

SHIFT SLIDE: Same as legato slide, except the second note is struck.

PINCH HARMONIC: The note is fretted normally and a harmonic is produced by adding the edge of the thumb or the tip of the index finger of the pick hand to the normal pick attack.

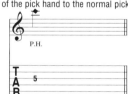

RAKE: Drag the pick across the strings indicated with a single motion.

VIBRATO BAR DIP: Strike the note and then immediately drop a specified number of steps, then release back to the original pitch.

THE HOTTEST TAB SONGBOOKS AVAILABLE FOR GUITAR & BASS!

PLAY IT LIKE IT IS GUITAR — WITH TABLATURE — NOTE-FOR-NOTE TRANSCRIPTIONS

PLAY IT LIKE IT IS BASS — WITH TABLATURE — NOTE-FOR-NOTE TRANSCRIPTIONS

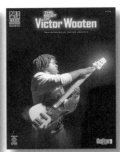

from

cherry lane music company

Guitar Transcriptions

02500702	Best of Black Label Society	$22.95
02500842	Black Label Society – Mafia	$19.95
02500116	Black Sabbath – Riff by Riff	$14.95
02500882	Blues Masters by the Bar	$19.95
02500921	Best of Joe Bonamassa	$22.95
02501272	Bush – 16 Stone	$21.95
02500179	Mary Chapin Carpenter Authentic Guitar Style of	$16.95
02500336	Eric Clapton – Just the Riffs	$12.99
02500684	Dashboard Confessional – A Mark • A Mission • A Brand • A Scar	$19.95
02500689	Dashboard Confessional – The Places You Have Come to Fear the Most	$17.95
02500843	Dashboard Confessional – The Swiss Army Romance	$17.95
02501481	Brett Dennen – So Much More	$19.99
02506878	John Denver Anthology for Easy Guitar Revised Edition	$15.95
02506901	John Denver Authentic Guitar Style	$14.95
02500984	John Denver – Folk Singer	$19.95
02506928	John Denver – Greatest Hits for Fingerstyle Guitar	$14.95
02500632	John Denver Collection Strum & Sing Series	$9.95
02501448	Best of Ronnie James Dio	$22.99
02500607	The Best of Dispatch	$19.95
02500198	Best of Foreigner	$19.95
02500990	Donavon Frankenreiter	$19.95
02501242	Guns N' Roses – Anthology	$24.95
02506953	Guns N' Roses – Appetite for Destruction	$22.95
02501286	Guns N' Roses Complete, Volume 1	$24.95
02501287	Guns N' Roses Complete, Volume 2	$24.95
02506211	Guns N' Roses – 5 of the Best, Vol. 1	$12.95
02506975	Guns N' Roses – GN'R Lies	$19.95
02500299	Guns N' Roses – Live Era '87-'93 Highlights	$24.95
02501193	Guns N' Roses – Use Your Illusion I	$24.99
02501194	Guns N' Roses – Use Your Illusion II	$24.95
02506325	Metallica – The Art of Kirk Hammett	$17.95
02500939	Hawthorne Heights – The Silence in Black and White	$19.95
02500458	Best of Warren Haynes	$22.95
02500476	Warren Haynes – Guide to Slide Guitar	$17.95
02500387	Best of Heart	$19.95
02500016	The Art of James Hetfield	$17.95
02500007	Hole – Celebrity Skin	$19.95
02500873	Jazz for the Blues Guitarist	$14.95
02500554	Jack Johnson – Brushfire Fairytales	$19.95
02500831	Jack Johnson – In Between Dreams	$19.95
02500653	Jack Johnson – On and On	$19.95
02501139	Jack Johnson – Sleep Through the Static	$19.95

02500858	Jack Johnson – Strum & Sing	$10.95
02501564	Jack Johnson – To the Sea	$19.99
02500380	Lenny Kravitz – Greatest Hits	$19.95
02500024	Best of Lenny Kravitz	$19.95
02500129	Adrian Legg – Pickin' 'n' Squintin'	$19.95
02500362	Best of Little Feat	$19.95
02501094	Hooks That Kill – The Best of Mick Mars & Mötley Crüe	$19.95
02500305	Best of The Marshall Tucker Band	$19.95
02501077	Dave Matthews Band – Anthology	$24.99
02501357	Dave Matthews Band – Before These Crowded Streets	$19.95
02500553	Dave Matthews Band – Busted Stuff	$22.95
02501279	Dave Matthews Band – Crash	$19.95
02500389	Dave Matthews Band – Everyday	$19.95
02501266	Dave Matthews Band – Under the Table and Dreaming	$19.95
02500131	Dave Matthews/Tim Reynolds – Live at Luther College, Vol. 1	$19.95
02500611	Dave Matthews/Tim Reynolds – Live at Luther College, Vol. 2	$22.95
02501502	John Mayer – Battle Studies	$22.99
02500986	John Mayer – Continuum	$22.99
02500705	John Mayer – Heavier Things	$22.95
02500529	John Mayer – Room for Squares	$22.95
02506965	Metallica – ...And Justice for All	$22.99
02501267	Metallica – Death Magnetic	$24.95
02506210	Metallica – 5 of the Best/Vol.1	$12.95
02506235	Metallica – 5 of the Best/Vol. 2	$12.95
02500070	Metallica – Garage, Inc.	$24.95
02507018	Metallica – Kill 'Em All	$19.99
02501232	Metallica – Live: Binge & Purge	$19.95
02501275	Metallica – Load	$24.95
02501195	Metallica – Metallica	$22.95
02501297	Metallica – ReLoad	$24.95
02507019	Metallica – Ride the Lightning	$19.95
02500279	Metallica – S&M Highlights	$24.95
02500638	Metallica – St. Anger	$24.95
02500577	Molly Hatchet – 5 of the Best	$9.95
02500846	Best of Steve Morse Band and Dixie Dregs	$19.95
02500765	Jason Mraz – Waiting for My Rocket to Come	$19.95
02501324	Jason Mraz – We Sing, We Dance, We Steal Things.	$22.99
02500448	Best of Ted Nugent	$19.95
02500707	Ted Nugent – Legendary Licks	$19.95
02500844	Best of O.A.R. (Of a Revolution)	$22.95
02500348	Ozzy Osbourne – Blizzard of Ozz	$19.95
02501277	Ozzy Osbourne – Diary of a Madman	$19.95
02507904	Ozzy Osbourne/Randy Rhoads Tribute	$22.95

02500524	The Bands of Ozzfest	$16.95
02500680	Don't Stop Believin': The Steve Perry Anthology	$22.95
02500025	Primus Anthology – A-N (Guitar/Bass)	$19.95
02500091	Primus Anthology – O-Z (Guitar/Bass)	$19.95
02500468	Primus – Sailing the Seas of Cheese	$19.95
02500875	Queens of the Stone Age – Lullabies to Paralyze	$24.95
02500608	Queens of the Stone Age – Songs for the Deaf	$19.95
02500659	The Best of Bonnie Raitt	$24.95
02501268	Joe Satriani	$22.95
02501299	Joe Satriani – Crystal Planet	$24.95
02500306	Joe Satriani – Engines of Creation	$22.95
02501205	Joe Satriani – The Extremist	$22.95
02507029	Joe Satriani – Flying in a Blue Dream	$22.95
02501155	Joe Satriani – Professor Satchafunkilus and the Musterion of Rock	$24.95
02500544	Joe Satriani – Strange Beautiful Music	$22.95
02500920	Joe Satriani – Super Colossal	$22.95
02506959	Joe Satriani – Surfing with the Alien	$19.95
02500560	Joe Satriani Anthology	$24.99
02501255	Best of Joe Satriani	$19.95
02501238	Sepultura – Chaos A.D.	$19.95
02500188	Best of the Brian Setzer Orchestra	$19.95
02500985	Sex Pistols – Never Mind the Bollocks, Here's the Sex Pistols	$19.95
02501230	Soundgarden – Superunknown	$19.95
02500799	Tenacious D	$19.95
02501035	Tenacious D – The Pick of Destiny	$19.95
02501263	Tesla – Time's Making Changes	$19.95
02501147	30 Easy Spanish Guitar Solos	$14.99
02500561	Learn Funk Guitar with Tower of Power's Jeff Tamelier	$19.95
02501007	Keith Urban – Love, Pain & The Whole Crazy Thing	$24.95
02500636	The White Stripes – Elephant	$19.95
02501095	The White Stripes – Icky Thump	$19.95
02500583	The White Stripes – White Blood Cells	$19.95
02501092	Wilco – Sky Blue Sky	$22.95
02500431	Best of Johnny Winter	$19.95
02500949	Wolfmother	$22.95
02500199	Best of Zakk Wylde	$22.99
02500700	Zakk Wylde – Legendary Licks	$19.95

Bass Transcriptions

02501108	Bass Virtuosos	$19.95
02500117	Black Sabbath – Riff by Riff Bass	$17.95
02506966	Guns N' Roses – Appetite for Destruction	$19.95
02501522	John Mayer Anthology for Bass, Vol. 1	$24.99
02500639	Metallica – St. Anger	$19.95
02500771	Best of Rancid for Bass	$17.95
02501120	Best of Tower of Power for Bass	$19.95
02500317	Victor Wooten Songbook	$22.95

Transcribed Scores

02500424	The Best of Metallica	$24.95
02500715	Mr. Big – Greatest Hits	$24.95
02500883	Mr. Big – Lean into It	$24.95

See your local music dealer or contact:

cherry lane music company

EXCLUSIVELY DISTRIBUTED BY
HAL•LEONARD CORPORATION
7777 W. BLUEMOUND RD. P.O. BOX 13819 MILWAUKEE, WI 53213

Prices, contents, and availability subject to change without notice.

0810